Presented to

_____

By

_____

On the Occasion of

_____

Date

_____

GOD from A to Z

Selected Bible Verses
for Knowing Him Better

Amy Ng Wong

BARBOUR
PUBLISHING, INC.
Uhrichsville, Ohio

GOD
from A to Z

Scripture quotations marked KJV are taken from the King James Version of the Bible. Scripture quotations marked NKJV are taken from the New King James Version. Copyright © 1979, 1980, 1982 by Thomas Nelson, Inc. Used by permission. All rights reserved. Scripture quotations marked RSV are from the Revised Standard Version of the Bible, copyright 1946, 1952, 1971 by the Division of Christian Education of the National Council of the Churches of Christ in the USA. Used by permission. Scripture quotations marked NRSV are taken from the New Revised Standard Version Bible, copyright 1989, Division of Christian Education of the National Council of the Churches of Christ in the United States of America. Used by permission. All rights reserved. Scripture quotations marked NIV are taken from the HOLY BIBLE, NEW INTERNATIONAL VERSION®. NIV®. Copyright © 1973, 1978, 1984 by International Bible Society. Used by permission of Zondervan Publishing House. All rights reserved. Scripture quotations marked TLB are taken from *The Living Bible* copyright © 1971. Used by permission of Tyndale House Publishers, Inc., Wheaton, Illinois 60189. All rights reserved. Scripture quotations marked NLT are taken from the *Holy Bible,* New Living Translation, copyright © 1996. Used by permission of Tyndale House Publishers, Inc. Wheaton, Illinois 60189, U.S.A. All rights reserved. Scripture quotations marked CEV are taken from the Contemporary English Version © 1991, 1992, 1995 by American Bible Society. Used by permission. Scripture quotations marked BBE are from the Bible in Basic English, © 1949, 1962 by C. K. Ogden and Cambridge University Press. Scripture quotations marked DV are taken from the Darby English Bible by John Nelson Darby, 1890. Scripture quotations marked YLT are taken from Young's Literal Translation by Robert Young, 1898.

Published by Barbour Publishing, Inc., P.O. Box 719, Uhrichsville, Ohio 44683 http://www.barbourbooks.com

Member of the
Evangelical Chri:
Publishers Assoc

Printed in the United States of America.

Acknowledgments

- Thank you, JoAnn Hedges, of BSF International, for persevering in sharing your love for such a wonderful God.

- Thank you, Kathryn Johnson, for the idea of listing God's attributes from A to Z.

- Thank you, David Hoffman, Bill Reed, and Chris Barnhill, for your encouragement and support in starting this book.

- Thank you, Michael Sanko, for so generously sharing your resources.

- Thank you, Yanni Zacharakis, for your insights of the original Greek meanings.

- Thank You, O Lord God Almighty, my everlasting Father, whom I love, for teaching me about Yourself even as I was compiling this book! Thank You for reaching down to rescue me in my times of need, for being such an amazing strategist in even the details of my life. I love You.

Contents

Incredible • Indispensable • Infinite • Instructor •
Intimate • Intolerant of Sin • Invisible

Preface

*Awesome, Beautiful, Counselor, Deliverer, Encourager,
Forgiving, Gentle, Helper, Incredible, Just, Kind, Leader,
Merciful, Near, Overcoming, Patient, Quiet, Righteous,
Sympathetic, True, Unchanging, Victorious, Wise,
Xristos, Yearning, Zealous*

If I knew a man with these attributes—or even just a
few of them—I would fall head over heels, completely
and absolutely in love with him! I would want to
marry him. Any man who might know a woman with
some of these attributes would want to marry her.

There is a Person who exhibits every one of these
qualities—God. And if we love the Lord our God
with all our heart, soul, and strength, we will marry
that perfect person—because God the Son, Jesus
Christ will be the bridegroom and we will be His
bride (see Matthew 25:1–10, Revelation 19:7–8)!

This book contains hundreds of Bible verses that
describe the character qualities, or attributes, of God.
You'll be amazed as you meet Him in all His power,
glory, and love—as you meet God, from A to Z.

Note: The verses used in this book have been carefully selected from a number of Bible translations—
whichever translation best brought out the attribute

of God under consideration. In some Bible versions, "thee," "thou," and "thine" mean "you" and "yours." "Ye" means "you." In this book, *italicized type* indicates material added by the author to clarify or explain Bible passages.

Absolute
See "Incomparable," "Omnipotent," "Sovereign."

Among the gods there is none like You, O Lord; nor are there any works like Your works. All nations whom You have made shall come and worship before You, O Lord, and shall glorify Your name. For You are great, and do wondrous things; You alone are God.

PSALM 86:8–10 NKJV

Almighty

"We cannot imagine the power of the Almighty, yet he is so just and merciful that he does not oppress us."

JOB 37:23 NLT

"Ah, Lord Jehovah, lo, Thou hast made the heavens and the earth by Thy great power, and by Thy stretched-out arm; there is nothing too wonderful for Thee: Doing kindness to thousands, and recompensing iniquity of fathers into the bosom of their sons after them; God, the great, the mighty, Jehovah of Hosts [is] His name, Great in counsel, and mighty in act, in that Thine eyes are open on all the ways of the sons of Adam, to give to each according to his ways, and according to the fruit of his doings."

JEREMIAH 32:17–19 YLT

15

"I am the Alpha and the Omega—the beginning and the end," says the Lord God. "I am the one who is, who always was, and who is still to come, the Almighty One."   REVELATION 1:8 NLT

"I [am] God Almighty, walk habitually before Me, and be thou perfect."   GENESIS 17:1 YLT

Amazing

Who is like unto thee, O LORD, among the gods? who is like thee, glorious in holiness, fearful in praises, doing wonders?   EXODUS 15:11 KJV

"The Almighty is beyond our reach and exalted in power; in his justice and great righteousness, he does not oppress."   JOB 37:23 NIV

Awesome

All heaven will praise your miracles, LORD; myriads of angels will praise you for your faithfulness. For who in all of heaven can compare with the LORD? What mightiest angel is anything like the LORD? The highest angelic powers stand in awe of God. He is far more awesome than those who surround his throne.

PSALM 89:5–7 NLT

I will meditate on the glorious splendor of Your majesty, And on Your wondrous works. Men shall speak of the might of Your awesome acts, And I will declare Your greatness.   PSALM 145:5–6 NKJV

"Out of the north he comes in golden splendor; God comes in awesome majesty."   JOB 37:22 NIV

"I pray, Lord God of heaven, O great and awesome God, You who keep Your covenant and mercy with those who love You and observe Your commandments."
                                                              NEHEMIAH 1:5 NKJV

Come, see the glorious things God has done. What marvelous miracles happen to his people!
                                                              PSALM 66:5 TLB

Beautiful

For the Holy Spirit, God's gift, does not want you to be afraid of people, but to be wise and strong, and to love them and enjoy being with them.
                                                              2 TIMOTHY 1:7 TLB

His glory covered the heavens and his praise filled the earth. His splendor was like the sunrise; rays flashed from his hand, where his power was hidden.
                                                              HABAKKUK 3:3–4 NIV

Blameless
See "Incorruptible," "Perfect," "Truth."

For the name of Jehovah will I proclaim: Ascribe greatness unto our God! [He is] the Rock, his work is perfect, For all his ways are righteousness; A God of faithfulness without deceit, Just and right is he.

DEUTERONOMY 32:3–4 DV

Boundless
See "Eternal," "Everlasting," "Omnipotent," "Omnipresent," "Omniscient."

There is no limit to God's existence in time or in distance. He is infinite in all directions, in the vastness of the entire universe as well as in the smallest neutron inside a molecule. He existed before the beginning of time, is here now, and will be after the end of time. There is no limit to His power, or to His knowledge, or to His existence. He has no bounds.

Canst thou by searching find out God? canst thou find out the Almighty unto perfection? It is as high as heaven; what canst thou do? deeper than hell; what canst thou know? The measure thereof is longer than the earth, and broader than the sea. If he cut off, and shut up, or gather together, then who can hinder him?

JOB 11:7–10 KJV

Builder

For every house is builded by some man; but he that built all things is God.   HEBREWS 3:4 KJV

For of Him and through Him and to Him are all things, to whom be glory forever.   ROMANS 11:36 NKJV

Caring

Casting all your care upon him; for he careth for you.
                                                    1 PETER 5:7 KJV

But I call to God, and the LORD saves me. Evening, morning and noon I cry out in distress, and he hears my voice. He ransoms me unharmed from the battle waged against me, even though many oppose me. God, who is enthroned forever, will hear them and afflict them— men who never change their ways and have no fear of God. Cast your cares on the LORD and he will sustain you; he will never let the righteous fall.

                                        PSALM 55:16–19, 22 NIV

Then they cried to the Lord in their troubles, and he rescued them! He led them from the darkness and shadow of death and snapped their chains. Oh, that

19

these men would praise the Lord for his loving-kindness and for all of his wonderful deeds!

PSALM 107:13–15 TLB

(God,) Which made heaven, and earth, the sea, and all that therein is: which keepeth truth for ever: Which executeth judgment for the oppressed: which giveth food to the hungry. The LORD looseth the prisoners: The LORD openeth the eyes of the blind: the LORD raiseth them that are bowed down: the LORD loveth the righteous: The LORD preserveth the strangers; he relieveth the fatherless and widow: but the way of the wicked he turneth upside down.

PSALM 146:6–9 KJV

As for your birth, on the day of your birth your cord was not cut and you were not washed in water to make you clean; you were not salted or folded in linen bands. No eye had pity on you to do any of these things to you or to be kind to you; but you were put out into the open country, because your life was hated at the time of your birth. And when I went past you and saw you stretched out in your blood, I said to you, Though you are stretched out in your blood, have life; And be increased in number like the buds of the field; and you were increased and became great, and you came to the time of love: your breasts were formed and your hair was long; but you were uncovered and without clothing. Now when I went past you, looking at you, I saw that your time was the time of love; and I put my skirts over you, covering your unclothed body: and I gave you my oath and made an agreement with you, says the Lord, and you became mine. Then I had you washed with water, washing away all your blood and rubbing you with oil. And I had you clothed with needlework, and put leather shoes on your feet, folding fair linen about you and covering you with silk. And I made you fair with ornaments and put jewels on your hands and a chain on your neck. And I put a ring in your nose and ear-rings in your ears and a beautiful crown on your head. So you were made beautiful with gold and silver; and your clothing was of the best linen and silk and needlework; your food was the best meal and honey and oil: and you were very beautiful. You were so beautiful that the story of you went out into all nations; you were completely beautiful because of my glory which I had put on you, says the Lord.   EZEKIEL 16:4–14 BBE

Christ

God's son, God's greatest expression of love for us even while we were yet sinners.

For God so loved the world, that he gave his only-begotten Son, that whosoever believes on him may not perish, but have life eternal.   JOHN 3:16 DV

Christ carried the burden of our sins. He was nailed to the cross, so that we would stop sinning and start living right. By his cuts and bruises you are healed.

1 PETER 2:24 CEV

God made him who had no sin *(Jesus Christ)* to be sin for us, so that in him we might become the righteousness of God. 2 CORINTHIANS 5:21 NIV

And as Moses lifted up the serpent in the wilderness, even so must the Son of Man *(also known as the Son of God)* be lifted up, that whoever believes in Him should not perish but have eternal life. JOHN 3:14-15 NKJV

"The Son of Man must be lifted up" means that Jesus had to be lifted up on the cross and suspended between heaven and earth; He had to be crucified. When Moses was leading the Israelites through the desert and many people were dying from poisonous snakebites, they could be saved by looking to the snake which was lifted up on Moses' staff— an image that is still today's medical symbol! Now, everyone who looks to Jesus on the cross, where He took our sins onto Himself, is saved and will not die. Jesus had to be sacrificed for our sins in order to pay our sin penalty, to make it possible for us to have eternal life.

He that believeth and is baptized shall be saved; but he that believeth not shall be damned.

MARK 16:16 KJV

. . .and from Jesus Christ, the faithful witness, the first-born from the dead, and the ruler over the kings of the earth. To Him who loved us and washed us from our sins in His own blood. . .   REVELATION 1:5 NKJV

For Christ also hath once suffered for sins, the just for the unjust, that he might bring us to God, being put to death in the flesh, but quickened by the Spirit.

1 PETER 3:18 KJV

Take heed, therefore, to yourselves, and to all the flock, among which the Holy Spirit made you over-seers, to feed the assembly of God that He acquired through His own blood.   ACTS 20:28 YLT

And they sang a new song, saying, "Worthy art thou *(Jesus)* to take the scroll and to open its seals, for thou wast slain and by thy blood didst ransom men for God from every tribe and tongue and people and nation."

REVELATION 5:9 RSV

For God in all his fullness was pleased to live in Christ.

COLOSSIANS 1:19 NLT

But God showed his great love for us by sending Christ to die for us while we were still sinners.

ROMANS 5:8 TLB

Comforter

Blessed be the God and Father of our Lord Jesus Christ, the Father of mercies and God of all comfort, who comforts us in all our tribulation, that we may be able to comfort those who are in any trouble, with the comfort with which we ourselves are comforted by God.

2 CORINTHIANS 1:3–4 NKJV

Because You, Lord, have helped me and comforted me. . .

PSALM 86:17 NKJV

"As a mother comforts her child, so will I comfort you; and you will be comforted over Jerusalem."

ISAIAH 66:13 NIV

"Can a mother forget the baby at her breast and have no compassion on the child she has borne? Though she may forget, I will not forget you!"

ISAIAH 49:15 NIV

The righteous cry, and the LORD heareth, and delivereth them out of all their troubles. The LORD is nigh unto them that are of a broken heart; and saveth such as be of a contrite spirit. Many are the afflictions of the righteous: but the LORD delivereth him out of them all. He keepeth all his bones: not one of them is broken. Evil shall slay the wicked: and they that hate the righteous shall be desolate. The LORD redeemeth the soul of his servants: and none of them that trust in him shall be desolate.

PSALM 34:17–22 KJV

I, even I *(the LORD),* am he that comforteth you: who art thou, that thou shouldest be afraid of a man that shall die, and of the son of man which shall be made as grass; And forgettest the LORD thy maker, that hath stretched forth the heavens, and laid the foundations of the earth; and hast feared continually every day because of the fury of the oppressor, as if he were ready to destroy? and where is the fury of the oppressor? The captive exile hasteneth that he may be loosed, and that he should not die in the pit, nor that his bread should fail. But I am the LORD thy God, that divided the sea, whose waves roared: The LORD of hosts is his name. And I have put my words in thy mouth, and I have covered thee in the shadow of mine hand, that I may plant the heavens, and lay the foundations of the earth, and say unto Zion, Thou art my people.

ISAIAH 51:12–16 KJV

The Lord, your God, is in your midst, a warrior who gives victory; he will rejoice over you with gladness, he will renew you in his love; he will exult over you with loud singing. ZEPHANIAH 3:17 NRSV

Compassionate

Your compassion is great, O LORD.

PSALM 119:156 NIV

The Lord is good to all, and his compassion is over all that he has made. PSALM 145:9 NRSV

"The LORD, the LORD, the compassionate and gracious God, slow to anger, abounding in love and faithfulness, maintaining love to thousands *(of those who love Me and keep My commandments, Exodus 20:6)*, and forgiving wickedness, rebellion and sin."

EXODUS 34:6–7 NIV

All praise to the God and Father of our Lord Jesus Christ. He is the source of every mercy and the God who comforts us. He comforts us in all our troubles so that we can comfort others. When others are troubled, we will be able to give them the same comfort God has given us. 2 CORINTHIANS 1:3–4 NLT

When God saw what they did and how they turned from their evil ways, he had compassion and did not bring upon them the destruction he had threatened.

JONAH 3:10 NIV

But the Lord was gracious to the people of Israel, and they were not totally destroyed. For God pitied them.

2 KINGS 13:23 TLB

Although God gives him grief, yet he will show compassion too, according to the greatness of His lovingkindness. For he does not enjoy afflicting men and causing sorrow.

LAMENTATIONS 3:32–33 TLB

Likewise the Spirit *(the Holy Spirit of God)* also helps in our weaknesses. For we do not know what we should pray for as we ought, but the Spirit Himself makes intercession for us with groanings which cannot be uttered.

ROMANS 8:26 NKJV

With dread deeds and awesome power you will defend us from our enemies, O God who saves us. You are the only hope of all mankind throughout the world and far away upon the sea.

PSALM 65:5 TLB

LORD, what are mortals that you should notice us, mere humans that you should care for us? For we are like a breath of air; our days are like a passing shadow.

PSALM 144:3–4 NLT

Consistent

And those who know Your name will put their trust in You; For You, Lord, have not forsaken those who seek You.   PSALM 9:10 NKJV

I the LORD do not change.   MALACHI 3:6 NRSV

Jesus Christ is the same yesterday, today, and forever.
                                                HEBREWS 13:8 NKJV

Counselor

"I will lead the blind by ways they have not known, along unfamiliar paths I will guide them; I will turn the darkness into light before them and make the rough places smooth."   ISAIAH 42:16 NIV

Trust in the LORD with all your heart; do not depend on your own understanding. Seek his will in all you do, and he will direct your paths.   PROVERBS 3:5–6 NLT

"But when the Father sends the Comforter instead of me—and by the Comforter I mean the Holy Spirit—he will teach you much, as well as remind you of everything I myself have told you."   JOHN 14:26 TLB

I will bless the Lord who counsels me; he gives me wisdom in the night. He tells me what to do.

PSALM 16:7 TLB

Hear, O my son, and receive my sayings; and the years of thy life shall be many. I have taught thee in the way of wisdom; I have led thee in right paths. When thou goest, thy steps shall not be straitened; and when thou runnest, thou shalt not stumble. Take fast hold of instruction; let her not go: keep her; for she is thy life. Enter not into the path of the wicked, and go not in the way of evil men. Avoid it, pass not by it, turn from it, and pass away. For they sleep not, except they have done mischief; and their sleep is taken away, unless they cause some to fall. For they eat the bread of wickedness, and drink the wine of violence. But the path of the just is as the shining light, that shineth more and more unto the perfect day. The way of the wicked is as darkness: they know not at what they stumble. My son, attend to my words; incline thine ear unto my sayings. Let them not depart from thine eyes; keep them in the midst of thine heart. For they are life unto those that find them, and health to all their flesh.

PROVERBS 4:10–22 KJV

"First seek the counsel of the LORD."   1 KINGS 22:5 NIV

Creator

For by him were all things created, that are in heaven, and that are in earth, visible and invisible, whether they be thrones, or dominions, or principalities, or powers: all things were created by him, and for him.

COLOSSIANS 1:16 KJV

"You alone are the LORD. You made the heavens, even the highest heavens, and all their starry host, the earth and all that is on it, the seas and all that is in them. You give life to everything, and the multitudes of heaven worship you."

NEHEMIAH 9:6 NIV

Praise ye the LORD. Praise ye the LORD from the heavens: praise him in the heights. Praise ye him, all his angels: praise ye him, all his hosts. Praise ye him, sun and moon: praise him, all ye stars of light. Praise him, ye heavens of heavens, and ye waters that be above the heavens. Let them praise the name of the LORD: for he commanded, and they were created.

PSALM 148:1–5 KJV

"You are worthy, our Lord and God, to receive glory and honor and power, for you created all things, and by your will they existed and were created."

REVELATION 4:11 NRSV

"Where wast thou when I laid the foundations of the earth? declare, if thou hast understanding. Who hath laid the measures thereof, if thou knowest? or who hath stretched the line upon it? Whereupon are the foundations thereof fastened? or who laid the corner stone thereof; When the morning stars sang together, and all the sons of God shouted for joy? Or who shut up the sea with doors, when it brake forth, as if it had issued out of the womb? When I made the cloud the garment thereof, and thick darkness a swaddlingband for it, and brake up for it my decreed place, and set bars and doors, and said, Hitherto shalt thou come, but no further: and here shall thy proud waves be stayed? Hast thou commanded the morning since thy days; and caused the dayspring to know his place; That it might take hold of the ends of the earth, that the wicked might be shaken out of it? It is turned as clay to the seal; and they stand as a garment. And from the wicked their light is withholden, and the high arm shall be broken. Hast thou entered into the springs of the sea? or hast thou walked in the search of the depth? Have the gates of death been opened unto thee? or hast thou seen the doors of the shadow of death? Hast thou perceived the breadth of the earth? declare if thou knowest it all. Where is the way where light dwelleth? and as for darkness, where is the place thereof, That thou shouldest take it to the bound thereof, and that thou shouldest know the paths to the house thereof? Knowest thou it,

31

because thou wast then born? or because the number of thy days is great? Hast thou entered into the treasures of the snow? or hast thou seen the treasures of the hail, Which I have reserved against the time of trouble, against the day of battle and war? By what way is the light parted, which scattereth the east wind upon the earth? Who hath divided a watercourse for the overflowing of waters, or a way for the lightning of thunder; To cause it to rain on the earth, where no man is; on the wilderness, wherein there is no man; To satisfy the desolate and waste ground; and to cause the bud of the tender herb to spring forth? Hath the rain a father? or who hath begotten the drops of dew? Out of whose womb came the ice? and the hoary frost of heaven, who hath gendered it? The waters are hid as with a stone, and the face of the deep is frozen. Canst thou bind the sweet influences of Pleiades, or loose the bands of Orion? Canst thou bring forth Mazzaroth in his season? or canst thou guide Arcturus with his sons? Knowest thou the ordinances of heaven? canst thou set the dominion thereof in the earth? Canst thou lift up thy voice to the clouds, that abundance of waters may cover thee? Canst thou send lightnings, that they may go and say unto thee, Here we are? Who hath put wisdom in the inward parts? or who hath given understanding to the heart? Who can number the clouds in wisdom? or who can stay the bottles of heaven, When the dust groweth into hardness, and the clods cleave fast together? Wilt thou hunt the prey for the lion? or fill the appetite of the young lions, When they couch in their dens, and abide in the covert to lie in wait? Who provideth for the raven his food? when his young ones cry unto God, they wander for lack of meat. Knowest thou the time when the wild goats of the rock bring forth? or canst thou mark when the hinds do calve? Canst thou number the months that they fulfil? or knowest thou the time when they bring forth? They bow themselves, they bring forth their young ones, they cast out their sorrows. Their young ones are in good liking, they grow up with corn; they go forth, and return not unto them. Who hath sent out the wild ass free? or who hath loosed the bands of the wild ass? Whose house I have made the wilderness, and the barren land his dwellings. He scorneth the multitude of the city, neither regardeth he the crying of the driver. The range of the mountains is his pasture, and he searcheth after every green thing. Will the unicorn be willing to serve thee, or abide by thy crib? Canst thou bind the unicorn with his band in the furrow? or will he harrow the valleys after thee? Wilt thou trust him, because his strength is great? or wilt thou leave thy labour to him? Wilt thou believe him, that he will bring home thy seed, and gather it into thy barn? Gavest thou the goodly wings unto the peacocks? or wings and feathers unto the ostrich? Which leaveth her eggs in the earth, and warmeth them in dust, And forgetteth

Defender

Their Defender is strong; he will take up their case.

PROVERBS 23:11 NIV

"The Lord will fight for you, and you won't need to lift a finger!"

EXODUS 14:14 TLB

I wait quietly before God, for my hope is in him. He alone is my rock and my salvation, my fortress where I will not be shaken. My salvation and my honor come from God alone. He is my refuge, a rock where no enemy can reach me.

PSALM 62:5–7 NLT

"No weapon formed against you shall prosper, And every tongue which rises against you in judgment You shall condemn. This is the heritage of the servants of the Lord, And their righteousness is from Me," Says the Lord.

ISAIAH 54:17 NKJV

"They will fight against you, But they shall not prevail against you. For I am with you," says the Lord, "to deliver you."

JEREMIAH 1:19 NKJV

Delightful
See "Joy," "Song."

Honour and majesty [are] before Him, Strength and joy [are] in His place.   1 CHRONICLES 16:27 YLT

Deliverer

I sought the LORD, and he heard me, and delivered me from all my fears.   PSALM 34:4 KJV

The angel of the Lord encamps all around those who fear Him, And delivers them.   PSALM 34:7 NKJV

The righteous cry out, and the Lord hears, And delivers them out of all their troubles. The Lord is near to those who have a broken heart, And saves such as have a contrite spirit. Many are the afflictions of the righteous, But the Lord delivers him out of them all. He guards all his bones; Not one of them is broken. Evil shall slay the wicked, And those who hate the righteous shall be condemned. The Lord redeems the soul of His servants, And none of those who trust in Him shall be condemned.   PSALM 34:17–22 NKJV

"I will cleanse you of your filthy behavior. I will give you good crops, and I will abolish famine in the land."   EZEKIEL 36:29 NLT

(The Lord is) My kind one, and my bulwark, My tower, and my deliverer, My shield, and in whom I have trusted, Who is subduing my people under me!

PSALM 144:2 YLT

Dependable

Lift up your eyes to the heavens, and look at the earth beneath; for the heavens will vanish like smoke, the earth will wear out like a garment, and those who live on it will die like gnats; but my salvation will be forever, and my deliverance will never be ended.

ISAIAH 51:6 NRSV

When you cry out, let your collection of idols deliver you! The wind will carry them off, a breath will take them away. But whoever takes refuge in me shall possess the land and inherit my holy mountain.

ISAIAH 57:13 NRSV

God is not a human being, that he should lie, or a mortal, that he should change his mind. Has he promised, and will he not do it? Has he spoken, and will he not fulfill it?

NUMBERS 23:19 NRSV

We know and rely on the love God has for us.

1 JOHN 4:16 NIV

Your word, O LORD, is eternal; it stands firm in the heavens. Your faithfulness continues through all generations; you established the earth, and it endures.

PSALM 119:89–90 NIV

"Behold, God is mighty, but despises no one; He is mighty in strength of understanding." JOB 36:5 NKJV

In spite of God's mighty power, power greater and more awesome than we can ever dream of, He is not condescending. We can depend on the fact that He loves us more than we can comprehend, and that He loves mercy and righteousness.

I will sing of the mercies of the LORD for ever: with my mouth will I make known thy faithfulness to all generations. For I have said, Mercy shall be built up for ever: thy faithfulness shalt thou establish in the very heavens.

PSALM 89:1–2 KJV

"For the mountains may depart and the hills disappear, but even then I will remain loyal to you. My covenant of blessing will never be broken," says the LORD, who has mercy on you.

ISAIAH 54:10 NLT

Diligent

"I will search. . .in darkest corners to find and punish those who sit contented in their sins, indifferent to God, thinking he will leave them alone."

ZEPHANIAH 1:12 TLB

For the eyes of the Lord range throughout the entire earth, to strengthen those whose heart is true to him.

2 CHRONICLES 16:9 NRSV

Discerning

But the LORD said to Samuel, "Do not consider his appearance or his height, for I have rejected him. The LORD does not look at the things man looks at. Man looks at the outward appearance, but the LORD looks at the heart."

1 SAMUEL 16:7 NIV

For a man's ways are in full view of the LORD, and he examines all his paths.

PROVERBS 5:21 NIV

The LORD's searchlight penetrates the human spirit, exposing every hidden motive.

PROVERBS 20:27 NLT

O Lord, thou hast searched me, and known me. Thou knowest my downsitting and mine uprising, thou understandest my thought afar off. Thou compassest my path and my lying down, and art acquainted with all my ways. For there is not a word in my tongue, but, lo, O LORD, thou knowest it altogether. Thou hast beset me behind and before, and laid thine hand upon me. Such knowledge is too wonderful for me; it is high, I cannot attain unto it. Whither shall I go from thy spirit? or whither shall I flee from thy presence? If I ascend up into heaven, thou art there: if I make my bed in hell, behold, thou art there. If I take the wings of the morning, and dwell in the uttermost parts of the sea; Even there shall thy hand lead me, and thy right hand shall hold me. If I say, Surely the darkness shall cover me; even the night shall be light about me. Yea, the darkness hideth not from thee; but the night shineth as the day: the darkness and the light are both alike to thee.   PSALM 139:1–12 KJV

"Get to know the God of your fathers. Worship and serve him with a clean heart and a willing mind, for the Lord sees every heart and understands and knows every thought. If you seek him, you will find him; but if you forsake him, he will permanently throw you aside."

1 CHRONICLES 28:9 TLB

Encourager

" 'Do not be afraid nor dismayed because of this great multitude, for the battle is not yours, but God's.' "

2 CHRONICLES 20:15 NKJV

Do not worry about anything, but in everything by prayer and supplication with thanksgiving let your requests be made known to God.   PHILIPPIANS 4:6 NRSV

Eternal

God existed before the foundation of the world. When the universe and the heavens vanish, God will remain.

"And do not forget the things I have done throughout history. For I am God—I alone! I am God, and there is no one else like me. Only I can tell you what is going to happen even before it happens. Everything I plan will come to pass, for I do whatever I wish."

ISAIAH 46:9–10 NLT

I am He; I am the first, and I am the last. My hand laid the foundation of the earth, and my right hand spread out the heavens; when I summon them, they stand at attention.   ISAIAH 48:12–13 NRSV

"I am the Alpha and the Omega—the Beginning and End—the First and the Last." REVELATION 22:13 YLT

The eternal God is your Refuge, And underneath are the everlasting arms. DEUTERONOMY 33:27 TLB

In the beginning, O Lord, you laid the foundations of the earth, and the heavens are the work of your hands. They will perish, but you remain; they will all wear out like a garment. You will roll them up like a robe; like a garment they will be changed. But you remain the same, and your years will never end.

HEBREWS 1:10–12 NIV

Evaluator

If ever you have among you a prophet or a dreamer of dreams and he gives you a sign or a wonder, And the sign or the wonder takes place, and he says to you, Let us go after other gods, which are strange to you, and give them worship; Then give no attention to the words of that prophet or that dreamer of dreams: for the Lord your God is testing you, to see if all the love of your heart and soul is given to him.

DEUTERONOMY 13:1–3 BBE

"For there will be many false Messiahs and false prophets who will do wonderful miracles that would deceive, if possible, even God's own children. Take care! I have warned you!" MARK 13:22–23 TLB

Beloved, do not believe every spirit, but test the spirits, whether they are of God; because many false prophets have gone out into the world. By this you know the Spirit of God: Every spirit that confesses that Jesus Christ has come in the flesh is of God, and every spirit that does not confess that Jesus Christ has come in the flesh is not of God. 1 JOHN 4:1–3 NKJV

"But He knows the way that I take; When He has tested me, I shall come forth as gold. My foot has held fast to His steps; I have kept His way and not turned aside. I have not departed from the commandment of His lips; I have treasured the words of His mouth more than my necessary food." JOB 23:10–12 NKJV

Everlasting

Do you not know? Have you not heard? The LORD is the everlasting God, the Creator of the ends of the earth. He will not grow tired or weary, and his understanding no one can fathom. ISAIAH 40:28 NIV

Before the mountains were brought forth, Or ever You had formed the earth and the world, Even from everlasting to everlasting, You are God.

PSALM 90:2 NKJV

"Holy, holy, holy, Lord God Almighty—the one who was, and is, and is to come." REVELATION 4:8 TLB

(God said), "I have loved you with an everlasting love; I have drawn you with loving-kindness."

JEREMIAH 31:3 NIV

Exalted

How awesome is the LORD Most High, the great King over all the earth! For the kings of the earth belong to God; he is greatly exalted. PSALM 47:2, 9 NIV

Yours, O Lord, are the greatness, the power, the glory, the victory, and the majesty; for all that is in the heavens and on the earth is yours; yours is the kingdom, O Lord, and you are exalted as head above all. Riches and honor come from you, and you rule over all. In your hand are power and might; and it is in your hand to make great and to give strength to all. And now, our God, we give thanks to you and praise your glorious name. 1 CHRONICLES 29:11–13 NRSV

"We cannot imagine the power of the Almighty, yet he is so just and merciful that he does not oppress us."

JOB 37:23 NLT

"See, God is exalted in his power; who is a teacher like him?"

JOB 36:22 NRSV

He makes wars cease to the ends of the earth; he breaks the bow and shatters the spear, he burns the shields with fire. "Be still, and know that I am God; I will be exalted among the nations, I will be exalted in the earth."

PSALM 46:9–10 NIV

Faith, Object of

What is faith? It is the confident assurance that what we hope for is going to happen. It is the evidence of things we cannot yet see.

HEBREWS 11:1 NLT

Faith is being sure of (the substance) what we hope for (our goal in Christ Jesus), and certain (the evidence) of what we do not see.

But without faith it is impossible to please Him, for he who comes to God must believe that He is, and that He is a rewarder of those who diligently seek Him.

HEBREWS 11:6 NKJV

Yet faith comes from listening to this message of good news—the Good News about Christ.

ROMANS 10:17 NLT

For by grace you have been saved through faith; and this is not your own doing, it is the gift of God.

EPHESIANS 2:8 RSV

We are made right in God's sight when we trust in Jesus Christ to take away our sins. And we all can be saved in this same way, no matter who we are or what we have done.

ROMANS 3:22 NLT

For indeed the good news came to us just as to them; but the message they heard did not benefit them, because they were not united by faith with those who listened.

HEBREWS 4:2 NRSV

He therefore that ministereth to you the Spirit, and worketh miracles among you, doeth he it by the works of the law, or by the hearing of faith? Even as Abraham believed God, and it was accounted to him for righteousness.

GALATIANS 3:5–6 KJV

No distrust made him waver concerning the promise of God, but he grew strong in his faith as he gave glory to God, being fully convinced that God was able to do what he had promised.

ROMANS 4:20–21 NRSV

So we fix our eyes not on what is seen, but on what is unseen. For what is seen is temporary, but what is unseen is eternal.   2 CORINTHIANS 4:18 NIV

For in it the righteousness of God is revealed through faith for faith; as it is written, "He who through faith is righteous shall live."   ROMANS 1:17 RSV

Faithful

The LORD is faithful to all his promises and loving toward all he has made.   PSALM 145:13 NIV

Those who know your name trust in you, for you, O LORD, have never abandoned anyone who searches for you.   PSALM 9:10 NLT

Your unfailing love will last forever. Your faithfulness is as enduring as the heavens.   PSALM 89:2 NLT

His faithfulness will be your shield and rampart.
     PSALM 91:4 NIV

"They will try, but they will fail. For I am with you," says the Lord. "I will deliver you."   JEREMIAH 1:19 TLB

Even if my father and mother abandon me, the LORD will hold me close.   PSALM 27:10 NLT

"I will never fail you. I will never forsake you" *(God promises to believers in Christ).*   HEBREWS 13:5 NLT

"Be strong and of good courage, do not fear nor be afraid of them; for the Lord your God, He is the One who goes with you. He will not leave you nor forsake you."   DEUTERONOMY 31:6 NKJV

But if we confess our sins to him, he can be depended on to forgive us and to cleanse us from every wrong. And it is perfectly proper for God to do this for us because Christ died to wash away our sins.

1 JOHN 1:9 TLB

"O LORD, God of heaven, the great and awesome God, who keeps his covenant of love with those who love him and obey his commands. . ."   NEHEMIAH 1:5 NIV

May God himself, the God of peace, sanctify you through and through. May your whole spirit, soul and body be kept blameless at the coming of our Lord Jesus Christ. The one who calls you is faithful and he will do it.   1 THESSALONIANS 5:23–24 NIV

Famous

LORD, I have heard of Your fame; I stand in awe of your deeds, O LORD.   HABAKKUK 3:2 NIV

"I am a great King," Says the LORD of hosts, "And My name is to be feared among the nations."

MALACHI 1:14 NKJV

You believe that there is one God. Good! Even the demons believe that—and shudder.   JAMES 2:19 NIV

Father

(The Lord's heart cry:) "I thought to myself, 'I would love to treat you as my own children!' I wanted nothing more than to give you this beautiful land—the finest inheritance in the world. I looked forward to your calling me 'Father,' and I thought you would never turn away from me again."   JEREMIAH 3:19 NLT

He destined us for adoption as his children through Jesus Christ, according to the good pleasure of his will, to the praise of his glorious grace that he freely bestowed on us in the Beloved.   EPHESIANS 1:5–6 NRSV

See how very much our heavenly Father loves us, for he allows us to be called his children, and we really are! But the people who belong to this world don't know God, so they don't understand that we are his children. Yes, dear friends, we are already God's children, and we can't even imagine what we will be like when Christ returns. But we do know that when he comes we will be like him, for we will see him as he really is. And all who believe this will keep themselves pure, just as Christ is pure. 1 JOHN 3:1–3 NLT

You are all sons of God through faith in Christ Jesus, for all of you who were baptized into Christ have clothed yourselves with Christ. There is neither Jew nor Greek, slave nor free, male nor female, for you are all one in Christ Jesus. GALATIANS 3:26–28 NIV

Every generous act of giving, with every perfect gift, is from above, coming down from the Father of lights, with whom there is no variation or shadow due to change. In fulfillment of his own purpose he gave us birth by the word of truth, so that we would become a kind of first fruits of his creatures. JAMES 1:17–18 NRSV

" 'You are my Father, my God, and the Rock of my salvation!' " PSALM 89:26 NRSV

My son, do not despise the LORD's discipline and do not resent his rebuke, because the LORD disciplines those he loves, as a father the son he delights in.

PROVERBS 3:11–12 NIV

He who spares the rod hates his son, but he who loves him is diligent to discipline him.   PROVERBS 13:24 RSV

(God said,) As many as I love, I rebuke and chasten.

REVELATION 3:19 KJV

And again, if the fathers of our flesh gave us punishment and had our respect, how much more will we be under the authority of the Father of spirits, and have life? For they truly gave us punishment for a short time, as it seemed good to them; but he does it for our profit, so that we may become holy as he is. At the time all punishment seems to be pain and not joy: but after, those who have been trained by it get from it the peace-giving fruit of righteousness.

HEBREWS 12:9–11 BBE

Fiery

The LORD went before them. . .a pillar of fire.

EXODUS 13:21 KJV

Thunder and lightning, . . .fire. . .the whole mountain trembled violently, . . . The LORD descended to the top of Mount Sinai.   EXODUS 19:16, 18, 20 NIV

Fire came out from the presence of the Lord and consumed them, and they died.   LEVITICUS 10:2 NRSV

Then the fire of the LORD fell, and consumed the burnt offering, and the wood, and the stones, and the dust, and licked up the water that was in the trench.

1 KINGS 18:38 RSV

Fire goes before him, and consumes his adversaries on every side. His lightnings light up the world; the earth sees and trembles. The mountains melt like wax before the Lord, before the Lord of all the earth.

PSALM 97:3–5 NRSV

Our God is a consuming fire.   HEBREWS 12:29 RSV

Then there appeared to them divided tongues, as of fire, and one sat upon each of them. And they were all filled with the Holy Spirit.   ACTS 2:3–4 NKJV

Out of the brightness of his presence bolts of lightning blazed forth.   2 SAMUEL 22:13 NIV

Firm

"God is mighty, but does not despise men; he is mighty, and firm in his purpose."   JOB 36:5 NIV

"My purpose shall stand, and I will fulfill my intention," . . . I have spoken, and I will bring it to pass; I have planned, and I will do it.   ISAIAH 46:10–11 NRSV

"Until heaven and earth disappear, not the smallest letter, not the least stroke of a pen, will by any means disappear from the Law until everything is accomplished."   MATTHEW 5:18 NIV

Till heaven and earth come to an end, not the smallest letter or part of a letter will in any way be taken from the law, till all things are done.   MATTHEW 5:18 BBE

Your love stands firm forever, . . .you established your faithfulness in heaven itself.   PSALM 89:2 NIV

The Lord preserves the faithful, but abundantly repays the one who acts haughtily.   PSALM 31:23 NRSV

"The LORD, the LORD, a God merciful and gracious, slow to anger, and abounding in steadfast love and faithfulness, keeping steadfast love for thousands, forgiving iniquity and transgression and sin, but who will by no means clear the guilty."   EXODUS 34:6–7 RSV

53

The LORD is slow to get angry, but his power is great, and he never lets the guilty go unpunished. He displays his power in the whirlwind and the storm. The billowing clouds are the dust beneath his feet. NAHUM 1:3 NLT

The LORD is good. When trouble comes, he is a strong refuge. And he knows everyone who trusts in him. But he sweeps away his enemies in an overwhelming flood. He pursues his foes into the darkness of night.

NAHUM 1:7–8 NLT

Forgiving

Who is a God like you, offering forgiveness for evil-doing and overlooking the sins of the rest of his heritage? he does not keep his wrath for ever, because his delight is in mercy. MICAH 7:18 BBE

Let the sinner give up his way, and the evil-doer his purpose: and let him come back to the Lord, and he will have mercy on him; and to our God, for there is full forgiveness with him. ISAIAH 55:7 BBE

And be kind to one another, tenderhearted, forgiving one another, as God in Christ forgave you.

EPHESIANS 4:32 RSV

Lord, if you keep in mind our sins, then who can ever

get an answer to his prayers? But you forgive! What an awesome thing this is! PSALM 130:3–4 TLB

I will heal their faithlessness; I will love them freely, for my anger has turned from them. HOSEA 14:4 RSV

"But they were disobedient and rebelled against you; they put your law behind their backs. They killed your prophets, who had admonished them in order to turn them back to you; they committed awful blasphemies. So you handed them over to their enemies, who oppressed them. But when they were oppressed they cried out to you. From heaven you heard them, and in your great compassion you gave them deliverers, who rescued them from the hand of their enemies. But as soon as they were at rest, they again did what was evil in your sight. Then you abandoned them to the hand of their enemies so that they ruled over them. And when they cried out to you again, you heard from heaven, and in your compassion you delivered them time after time."

NEHEMIAH 9:26–28 NIV

"I have blotted out, like a thick cloud, your transgressions, And like a cloud, your sins. Return to Me, for I have redeemed you." ISAIAH 44:22 NKJV

"I, even I, am He who blots out your transgressions for My own sake; And I will not remember your sins."

ISAIAH 43:25 NKJV

Fortress

Happy is he. . .Who says of the Lord, He is my safe place and my tower of strength: he is my God, in whom is my hope.   PSALM 91:1–2 BBE

Reverence for God gives a man deep strength; his children have a place of refuge and security.

PROVERBS 14:26 TLB

"The Lord is my rock and my fortress and my deliverer; The God of my strength, in whom I will trust; My shield and the horn of my salvation, My stronghold and my refuge; My Savior, You save me from violence. I will call upon the Lord, who is worthy to be praised; So shall I be saved from my enemies."

2 SAMUEL 22:2–4 NKJV

He is my loving ally and my fortress, my tower of safety, my deliverer. He stands before me as a shield, and I take refuge in him. He subdues the nations under me.   PSALM 144:2 NLT

Friend

The LORD confides in those who fear him *(who hate evil);* he makes his covenant known to them.

PSALM 25:14 NIV

(Jesus, God the Son, proclaims,) No longer do I give you the name of servants; because a servant is without knowledge of what his master is doing: I give you the name of friends, because I have given you knowledge of all the things which my Father has said to me.

JOHN 15:15 BBE

To fear the LORD is to hate evil.　　PROVERBS 8:13 NIV

All this has come to your ears and you have seen it; will you not give witness to it? I am now making clear new things, even secret things, of which you had no knowledge.　　ISAIAH 48:6 BBE

There are friends who pretend to be friends, but there is a friend who sticks closer than a brother.

PROVERBS 18:24 RSV

"Even now my witness is in heaven; my advocate is on high. My intercessor is my friend as my eyes pour out tears to God; on behalf of a man he pleads with God as a man pleads for his friend."　　JOB 16:19–21 NIV

"Kings shall stand at attention when you pass by; princes shall bow low because the Lord has chosen you; he, the faithful Lord, the Holy One of Israel, chooses you."　　ISAIAH 49:7 TLB

Generous

"And if the LORD is pleased with us, he will bring us safely into that land and give it to us. It is a rich land flowing with milk and honey, and he will give it to us!"

NUMBERS 14:8 NLT

Or which of you, if his son makes a request for bread, will give him a stone? Or if he makes a request for a fish, will give him a snake? If you, then, being evil, are able to give good things to your children, how much more will your Father in heaven give good things to those who make requests to him? MATTHEW 7:9–11 BBE

Since he did not spare even his own Son for us but gave him up for us all, won't he also surely give us everything else? ROMANS 8:32 TLB

"If you then, who are evil, know how to give good gifts to your children, how much more will the heavenly Father give the Holy Spirit to those who ask him!"

LUKE 11:13 NRSV

How we praise God, the Father of our Lord Jesus Christ, who has blessed us with every spiritual blessing in the heavenly realms because we belong to Christ.

EPHESIANS 1:3 NLT

He destined us in love to be his sons through Jesus Christ, according to the purpose of his will, to the praise of his glorious grace which he freely bestowed on us in the Beloved. In him we have redemption through his blood, the forgiveness of our trespasses, according to the riches of his grace which he lavished upon us.

EPHESIANS 1:5–8 RSV

Let it be all joy to you, my brothers, when you undergo tests of every sort; Because you have the knowledge that the testing of your faith gives you the power of going on in hope; But let this power have its full effect, so that you may be made complete, needing nothing. But if any man among you is without wisdom, let him make his request to God, who gives freely to all without an unkind word, and it will be given to him.

JAMES 1:2–5 BBE

"Ask, and it will be given you; search, and you will find; knock, and the door will be opened for you."

MATTHEW 7:7, LUKE 11:9 NRSV

Give, and it will be given to you; good measure, crushed down, full and running over, they will give to you. For in the same measure as you give, it will be given to you again.

LUKE 6:38 BBE

He who sows sparingly will also reap sparingly, and he who sows bountifully will also reap bountifully. Each one must do as he has made up his mind, not reluctantly or under compulsion, for God loves a cheerful giver.   2 CORINTHIANS 9:6–7 RSV

"Assuredly, I say to you, there is no one who has left house or parents or brothers or wife or children, for the sake of the kingdom of God, who shall not receive many times more in this present time, and in the age to come eternal life."   LUKE 18:29–30 NKJV

Gentle

But the fruit of the Spirit is love, joy, peace, a quiet mind, kind acts, well-doing, faith, Gentle behaviour, control over desires.   GALATIANS 5:22–23 BBE

Then a great and powerful wind tore the mountains apart and shattered the rocks before the LORD, but the LORD was not in the wind. After the wind there was an earthquake, but the LORD was not in the earthquake. After the earthquake came a fire, but the LORD was not in the fire. And after the fire came a gentle whisper.

1 KINGS 19:11–12 NIV

He tends his flock like a shepherd: He gathers the lambs in his arms and carries them close to his heart; he gently leads those that have young.   ISAIAH 40:11 NIV

But avoid foolish and ignorant disputes, knowing that they generate strife. And a servant of the Lord must not quarrel but be gentle to all, able to teach, patient, in humility correcting those who are in opposition, if God perhaps will grant them repentance, so that they may know the truth, and that they may come to their senses and escape the snare of the devil, having been taken captive by him to do his will.

2 TIMOTHY 2:23–26 NKJV

(Jesus teaches,) Take my yoke on you and become like me, for I am gentle and without pride, and you will have rest for your souls; For my yoke is good, and the weight I take up is not hard.   MATTHEW 11:29–30 BBE

Giver

You have given him his heart's desire, And have not withheld the request of his lips. Selah For You meet him with the blessings of goodness; You set a crown of pure gold upon his head.   PSALM 21:2–3 NKJV

Delight yourself in the LORD and he will give you the desires of your heart.   PSALM 37:4 NIV

He fulfils the desire of all who fear him, he also hears
their cry, and saves them.   PSALM 145:19 RSV

For God had such love for the world that he gave his
only Son, so that whoever has faith in him may not
come to destruction but have eternal life.

JOHN 3:16 BBE

We love Him because He first loved us.

1 JOHN 4:19 NKJV

*God longs to give us more than we can even imagine, if
we would only search for Him, then have the faith to obey
Him when we hear Him.*

Ah Lord GOD! behold, thou hast made the heaven and
the earth by thy great power and stretched out arm, and
there is nothing too hard for thee.

JEREMIAH 32:17 KJV

Glorifier

And having chosen us, he called us to come to him; and
when we came, he declared us "not guilty," filled us with
Christ's goodness, gave us right standing with himself,
and promised us his glory.   ROMANS 8:30 TLB

Glorious

"Great and amazing are your deeds, Lord God the Almighty! Just and true are your ways, King of the nations! Lord, who will not fear and glorify your name? For you alone are holy. All nations will come and worship before you, for your judgments have been revealed." REVELATION 15:3–4 NRSV

The heavens are telling the glory of God; they are a marvelous display of his craftsmanship.

PSALM 19:1 TLB

His glory covered the heavens and his praise filled the earth. His splendor was like the sunrise; rays flashed from his hand, where his power was hidden.

HABAKKUK 3:3–4 NIV

To him who is able to keep you from falling and to present you before his glorious presence without fault and with great joy. . . JUDE 24 NIV

Who is this King of glory? The Lord strong and mighty, The Lord mighty in battle. . . . Lift up, you everlasting doors! And the King of glory shall come in. Who is this King of glory? The Lord of hosts, He is the King of glory. PSALM 24:8–10 NKJV

The God of glory thunders. PSALM 29:3 RSV

God of gods

The king answered Daniel, and said, "Truly your God is the God of gods, the Lord of kings, and a revealer of secrets, since you could reveal this secret."

DANIEL 2:47 NKJV

Great is the LORD! He is most worthy of praise! He is to be revered above all gods. The gods of other nations are merely idols, but the LORD made the heavens!

1 CHRONICLES 16:25–26 NLT

For the LORD your God is God of gods and Lord of lords, the great God, mighty and awesome, who shows no partiality and accepts no bribes.

DEUTERONOMY 10:17 NIV

O give thanks to the God of gods, for his steadfast love endures for ever. PSALM 136:2 RSV

Good

For the Lord is good, and his mercy is never-ending; his faith is unchanging through all generations.

PSALM 100:5 BBE

Oh, put God to the test and see how kind he is! See for yourself the way his mercies shower down on all who trust in him. PSALM 34:8 TLB

O taste and see that the LORD is good! Happy is the man who takes refuge in him! PSALM 34:8 RSV

The LORD is good, a refuge in times of trouble. He cares for those who trust in him. NAHUM 1:7 NIV

For God cannot be tempted by evil, nor does he tempt anyone. JAMES 1:13 NIV

They shall celebrate the fame of your abundant goodness, and shall sing aloud of your righteousness.
PSALM 145:7 NRSV

You are good, and your works are good; give me knowledge of your rules. PSALM 119:68 BBE

"The LORD is upright; he is my Rock, and there is no wickedness in him." PSALM 92:15 NIV

Preserve me, O God, for in You I put my trust. O my soul, you have said to the Lord, "You are my Lord, My goodness is nothing apart from You."
PSALM 16:1–2 NKJV

For as you know him better, he will give you, through his great power, everything you need for living a truly good life: he even shares his own glory and his own goodness with us!   2 PETER 1:3 TLB

Oh, that these men would praise the Lord for his loving-kindness, and for all of his wonderful deeds! For he satisfies the thirsty soul and fills the hungry soul with good.   PSALM 107:8–9 TLB

" 'Yes, I will rejoice over them to do them good, and I will assuredly plant them in this land, with all My heart and with all My soul.' "

                    JEREMIAH 32:41 NKJV

"This is what the LORD Almighty says: 'Administer true justice; show mercy and compassion to one another. Do not oppress the widow or the fatherless, the alien or the poor. In your hearts do not think evil of each other.' "   ZECHARIAH 7:9–10 NIV

"Why ask me about what is good?" Jesus replied. "Only God is good. But to answer your question, you can receive eternal life if you keep the commandments."

                    MATTHEW 19:17 NLT

Gospel

Gospel means "good news." The good news that death, the penalty for our sins, can be avoided. Christ died for our penalty in our place, then arose from (conquered) death and lives today. We can be saved from our sin penalty by believing in Him, and asking Him into our hearts to be our Savior—asking Him to be the Lord of our lives; asking Him into our minds and hearts to replace our tendency to sin and selfishness.

By this gospel you are saved, if you hold firmly to the word I preached to you. . .that Christ died for our sins according to the Scriptures, that he was buried, that he was raised on the third day according to the Scriptures.

1 CORINTHIANS 15:2–4 NIV

And you, who once were alienated and enemies in your mind by wicked works, yet now He has reconciled in the body of His flesh through death, to present you holy, and blameless, and above reproach in His sight— if indeed you continue in the faith, grounded and steadfast, and are not moved away from the hope of the gospel which you heard, which was preached to every creature under heaven. COLOSSIANS 1:21–23 NKJV

Gracious

But You, O LORD, are a compassionate and gracious God, slow to anger, abounding in love and faithfulness.

PSALM 86:15 NIV

The LORD is gracious and merciful, slow to anger and abounding in steadfast love.

PSALM 145:8 RSV

The LORD longs to be gracious to you.

ISAIAH 30:18 NIV

Great

Truly, God is great, greater than all our knowledge.

JOB 36:26 BBE

And the house which I am building is to be great, for our God is greater than all gods. But who may have strength enough to make a house for him, seeing that the heaven and the heaven of heavens are not wide enough to be his resting-place? who am I then to make a house for him? But I am building it only for the burning of perfume before him.

2 CHRONICLES 2:5–6 BBE

O Lord, there is no other god like you. For you are great and your name is full of power.

JEREMIAH 10:6 TLB

You have done so much for me, O Lord. No wonder I am glad! I sing for joy. O Lord, what miracles you do! And how deep are your thoughts! PSALM 92:4–5 TLB

For you are great and perform great miracles. You alone are God. PSALM 86:10 NLT

Grievable

"Look around you and see if you can find another nation anywhere that has traded in its old gods for new ones—even though their gods are nothing. Send to the west to the island of Cyprus; send to the east to the deserts of Kedar. See if anyone there has ever heard so strange a thing as this. And yet my people have given up their glorious God for silly idols! The heavens are shocked at such a thing and shrink back in horror and dismay. For my people have done two evil things: They have forsaken me, the Fountain of Life-giving Water; and they have built for themselves broken cisterns that can't hold water!" JEREMIAH 2:10–13 TLB

The LORD was grieved that he had made man on the earth, and his heart was filled with pain.

GENESIS 6:6 NIV

But they rebelled against him and grieved his Holy Spirit. ISAIAH 63:10 TLB

Guide
See "Counselor" and "Teacher."

No one who trusts in you will ever be disgraced, but disgrace comes to those who try to deceive others. Show me the path where I should walk, O LORD; point out the right road for me to follow. Lead me by your truth and teach me, for you are the God who saves me. All day long I put my hope in you.

PSALM 25:3–5 NLT

Your word is a lamp to my feet and a light to my path.
PSALM 119:105 NRSV

My child, be attentive to my words; incline your ear to my sayings. Do not let them escape from your sight; keep them within your heart. For they are life to those who find them, and healing to all their flesh.

PROVERBS 4:20–22 NRSV

Trust in the LORD with all your heart, and do not rely on your own insight. In all your ways acknowledge him, and he will make straight your paths.

PROVERBS 3:5–6 RSV

Hater of idolatry
See "Jealous."

I am the Lord; that is my name: I will not give my glory to another, or my praise to pictured images.

ISAIAH 42:8 BBE

With part of it *(wood)* he makes a fire, and on the fire he gets meat cooked and takes a full meal: he makes himself warm, and says, Aha! I am warm, I have seen the fire: And the rest of it he makes into a god, even his pictured image: he goes down on his face before it, giving worship to it, and making prayer to it, saying, Be my saviour; for you are my god. They have no knowledge or wisdom; for he has put a veil over their eyes, so that they may not see; and on their hearts, so that they may not give attention. And no one takes note, no one has enough knowledge or wisdom to say, I have put part of it in the fire, and made bread on it; I have had a meal of the flesh cooked with it: and am I now to make the rest of it into a false god? am I to go down on my face before a bit of wood?

ISAIAH 44:16–19 BBE

Healer

O Lord my God, I cried out to You, And You healed me. O Lord, You brought my soul up from the grave; You have kept me alive, that I should not go down to the pit.   PSALM 30:2–3 NKJV

Then great multitudes came to Him, having with them the lame, blind, mute, maimed, and many others; and they laid them down at Jesus' feet, and He healed them. So the multitude marveled when they saw the mute speaking, the maimed made whole, the lame walking, and the blind seeing; and they glorified the God of Israel.   MATTHEW 15:30–31 NKJV

But he *(Jesus)* was wounded and crushed for our sins. He was beaten that we might have peace. He was whipped, and we were healed!   ISAIAH 53:5 NLT

"If you diligently heed the voice of the Lord your God and do what is right in His sight, give ear to His commandments and keep all His statutes, I will put none of the diseases on you which I have brought on the Egyptians. For I am the Lord who heals you."

EXODUS 15:26 NKJV

Be not wise in your own eyes; fear the LORD, and turn away from evil. It will be healing to your flesh and refreshment to your bones.   PROVERBS 3:7–8 RSV

Therefore confess your sins to one another, and pray for one another, so that you may be healed. The prayer of the righteous is powerful and effective. JAMES 5:16 NRSV

(The Lord Almighty says), "But for you who revere my name, the sun of righteousness will rise with healing in its wings." MALACHI 4:2 NIV

Heavenly

Every good and perfect gift is from above, coming down from the Father of the heavenly lights, who does not change like shifting shadows. JAMES 1:17 NIV

For who in the heavens can be compared to the Lord? Who among the sons of the mighty can be likened to the Lord? PSALM 89:6 NKJV

O LORD, our Lord, the majesty of your name fills the earth! Your glory is higher than the heavens.
PSALM 8:1 NLT

Praise the LORD, all his heavenly hosts, you his servants who do his will. PSALM 103:21 NIV

And the Lord will deliver me from every evil work and preserve me for His heavenly kingdom. To Him be glory forever and ever. 2 TIMOTHY 4:18 NKJV

Helper

I lift up my eyes to the hills—from where will my help come? My help comes from the Lord, who made heaven and earth.   PSALM 121:1–2 NRSV

In the day of my trouble I call on you, for you will answer me.   PSALM 86:7 NRSV

"Do not fear, for I am with you; do not be dismayed, for I am your God. I will strengthen you and help you; I will uphold you with my righteous right hand. . . . For I am the LORD, your God, who takes hold of your right hand and says to you, Do not fear; I will help you."   ISAIAH 41:10, 13 NIV

And in the same way—by our faith—the Holy Spirit helps us with our daily problems and in our praying. For we don't even know what we should pray for nor how to pray as we should; but the Holy Spirit prays for us with such feeling that it cannot be expressed in words.   ROMANS 8:26 TLB

For the eyes of the Lord search back and forth across the whole earth, looking for people whose hearts are perfect toward him, so that he can show his great power in helping them.   2 CHRONICLES 16:9 TLB

I will be your helper, says the Lord, even he who takes up your cause.   ISAIAH 41:14 BBE

After you have suffered a little while, our God, who is full of kindness through Christ, will give you his eternal glory. He personally will come and pick you up, and set you firmly in place, and make you stronger than ever.
          1 PETER 5:10 TLB

Holy

You are to be holy, for I, the Lord your God, am holy.
          LEVITICUS 19:2 BBE

Try to live in peace with everyone, and seek to live a clean and holy life, for those who are not holy will not see the Lord.   HEBREWS 12:14 NLT

Fear of the LORD is the beginning of wisdom. Knowledge of the Holy One results in understanding.
          PROVERBS 9:10 NLT

"How can I give you up?. . . How can I hand you over?. . . My heart is changed within me; all my compassion is aroused. I will not carry out my fierce anger, . . . For I am God, and not man—the Holy One among you. I will not come in wrath." HOSEA 11:8–9 NIV

Therefore prepare your minds for action; discipline yourselves; set all your hope on the grace that Jesus Christ will bring you when he is revealed. Like obedient children, do not be conformed to the desires that you formerly had in ignorance. Instead, as he who called you is holy, be holy yourselves in all your conduct; for it is written, "You shall be holy, for I am holy." 1 PETER 1:13–16 NRSV

Because the Lord your God travels along with your camp, to save you and to hand over your enemies to you, therefore your camp must be holy, so that he may not see anything indecent among you and turn away from you. DEUTERONOMY 23:14 NRSV

Exalt the Lord our God, And worship at His holy hill; For the Lord our God is holy. PSALM 99:9 NKJV

But the Lord of hosts is exalted by justice, and the Holy God shows himself holy by righteousness.

ISAIAH 5:16 NRSV

Give to the LORD the glory he deserves! Bring your offering and come to worship him. Worship the LORD in all his holy splendor. 1 CHRONICLES 16:29 NLT

"Holy, holy, holy, Lord God Almighty, Who was and is and is to come!" REVELATION 4:8 NKJV

Honest

Lord, who may dwell in your sanctuary? Who may live on your holy hill? He whose walk is blameless and who does what is righteous, who speaks the truth from his heart and has no slander on his tongue, who does his neighbor no wrong and casts no slur on his fellowman, who despises a vile man but honors those who fear the LORD, who keeps his oath even when it hurts, who lends his money without usury *(excessive interest)* and does not accept a bribe against the innocent.

PSALM 15:1–5 NIV

God, . . .cannot lie.   TITUS 1:2 NKJV

Hope

You are my hope, O Lord GOD.   PSALM 71:5 NKJV

Even youths grow tired and weary, and young men stumble and fall; but those who hope in the LORD will renew their strength. They will soar on wings like eagles; they will run and not grow weary, they will walk and not be faint.   ISAIAH 40:30–31 NIV

Oh how great is thy goodness, which thou hast laid up for them that fear thee; which thou hast wrought for them that trust in thee before the sons of men! Thou shalt hide them in the secret of thy presence from the pride of man: thou shalt keep them secretly in a pavilion from the strife of tongues. Blessed be the LORD: for he hath shewed me his marvelous kindness in a strong city. For I said in my haste, I am cut off from before thine eyes: nevertheless thou heardest the voice of my supplications when I cried unto thee. O love the LORD, all ye his saints: for the LORD preserveth the faithful, and plentifully rewardeth the proud doer. Be of good courage, and he shall strengthen your heart, all ye that hope in the LORD.   PSALM 31:19–24 KJV

Now may the God of hope make you full of joy and peace through faith, so that all hope may be yours in the power of the Holy Spirit.   ROMANS 15:13 BBE

But as for me, I watch in hope for the LORD, I wait for God my Savior; my God will hear me. Do not gloat over me, my enemy! Though I have fallen, I will rise. Though I sit in darkness, the LORD will be my light. Because I have sinned against him, I will bear the LORD's wrath, until he pleads my case and establishes my right. He will bring me out into the light; I will see his righteousness.   MICAH 7:7–9 NIV

And kings will take care of you, and queens will give you their milk: they will go down on their faces before you, kissing the dust of your feet; and you will be certain that I am the Lord, and that those who put their hope in me will not be shamed.

ISAIAH 49:23 BBE

You will give us an answer in righteousness by great acts of power, O God of our salvation; you who are the hope of all the ends of the earth, and of the far-off lands of the sea.   PSALM 65:5 BBE

Humble

"The Almighty is beyond our reach and exalted in power; in his justice and great righteousness, he does not oppress."   JOB 37:23 NIV

"God is mighty, but despises no one."   JOB 36:5 NKJV

And go nobly on in your power, because you are good and true and without pride.   PSALM 45:4 BBE

Let all of you put away pride and make yourselves ready to be servants: for God is a hater of pride, but he gives grace to those who make themselves low.

1 PETER 5:5 BBE

God chose what is foolish in the world to shame the wise, God chose what is weak in the world to shame the strong, God chose what is low and despised in the world, even things that are not, to bring to nothing things that are, so that no human being might boast in the presence of God.   1 CORINTHIANS 1:27–29 RSV

The high and lofty one who inhabits eternity, the Holy One, says this: "I live in that high and holy place with those whose spirits are contrite and humble. I refresh the humble and give new courage to those with repentant hearts.   ISAIAH 57:15 NLT

(God says,) "This is the one I esteem: he who is humble and contrite in spirit, and trembles at My word."

ISAIAH 66:2 NIV

If you do not have a change of heart and become like little children, you will not go into the kingdom of heaven. Whoever, then, will make himself as low as this little child, the same is the greatest in the kingdom of heaven. And whoever gives honour to one such little child in my name, gives honour to me.

MATTHEW 18:3–5 BBE

The Lord lifts up the humble; He casts the wicked down to the ground.   PSALM 147:6 NKJV

You rebuke those cursed proud ones who refuse your commands.   PSALM 119:21 TLB

The LORD detests all the proud of heart. Be sure of this: They will not go unpunished.   PROVERBS 16:5 NIV

Knowledge puffs up *(self)*, but love builds up *(others)*.
                    1 CORINTHIANS 8:1 NRSV

Even though God's knowledge is so vast that "the foolishness of God is wiser than man's wisdom" (1 Corinthians 1:25 NIV), He is without pride. His actions are only for building us up. He thinks of us and not of Himself. Jesus proves that. God is love. He does not think of self.

Illuminating

For you are my light, O Lord; and the Lord will make the dark bright for me.   2 SAMUEL 22:29 BBE

Your words are a flashlight to light the path ahead of me, and keep me from stumbling.   PSALM 119:105 TLB

"Truly, O Daniel," the king said, "your God is the God of gods, Ruler of kings, the Revealer of mysteries, because he has told you this secret."   DANIEL 2:47 TLB

And the Lord went before them by day in a pillar of cloud, guiding them on their way; and by night in a pillar of fire to give them light: so that they were able to go on day and night.   EXODUS 13:21 BBE

From the throne came flashes of lightning, rumblings and peals of thunder. Before the throne, seven lamps were blazing. These are the seven spirits of God.

REVELATION 4:5 NIV

Immortal

Now to the King eternal, immortal, invisible, to God who alone is wise, be honor and glory forever and ever.   1 TIMOTHY 1:17 NKJV

Claiming to be wise, they became fools; and they exchanged the glory of the immortal God for images resembling a mortal human being or birds or four-footed animals or reptiles.   ROMANS 1:22–23 NRSV

He alone can never die, and he lives in light so brilliant that no human can approach him. No one has ever seen him, nor ever will.   1 TIMOTHY 6:16 NLT

Immutable
See "Unchanging."

There can be no mutation in the character of God—He is perfection; He cannot be holier than He is, and He cannot deteriorate.

In the past you put the earth on its base, and the heavens are the work of your hands. They will come to an end, but you will still go on; they all will become old like a coat, and like a robe they will be changed: But you are the unchanging One, and your years will have no end.   PSALM 102:25–27 BBE

Every good and perfect gift is from above, coming down from the Father of the heavenly lights, who does not change like shifting shadows.   JAMES 1:17 NIV

Jesus Christ is the same yesterday and today and for ever.   HEBREWS 13:8 RSV

Impartial

"Who says to a king, 'Worthless one,' and to nobles, 'Wicked man'; who shows no partiality to princes, nor regards the rich more than the poor, for they are all the work of his hands?"   JOB 34:18–19 RSV

"He is not impressed by the world's wisest men!"

JOB 37:24 TLB

"God is mighty, yet he does not despise anyone! He is mighty in both power and understanding."

JOB 36:5 NLT

O Lord, what is man that you even notice him? Why bother at all with the human race? For man is but a breath; his days are like a passing shadow.

PSALM 144:3–4 TLB

"I now realize how true it is that God does not show favoritism but accepts men from every nation who fear him and do what is right." ACTS 10:34–35 NIV

But the wisdom that comes from heaven is first of all pure. It is also peace loving, gentle at all times, and willing to yield to others. It is full of mercy and good deeds. It shows no partiality and is always sincere.

JAMES 3:17 NLT

Incomparable

Among the gods there is none like you, O Lord; no deeds can compare with yours. For you are great and do marvelous deeds; you alone are God.

PSALM 86:8, 10 NIV

The Lord is perfect. Everything He says and thinks is truth, with no variation of the truth. He loves justice. He loves mercy. He is selfless—everything He does is for the good of others, not His own. He is not only full of love, He is love. He is so much better than we are in all areas of goodness that even our best acts of righteousness dingy and dirty compared to His radiant and pure righteousness.

All our righteousnesses are like filthy rags.

ISAIAH 64:6 NKJV

For who is there in the heavens in comparison with the Lord? who is like the Lord among the sons of the gods? God is greatly to be feared among the saints, and to be honoured over all those who are about him. O Lord God of armies, who is strong like you, O Jah? and your unchanging faith is round about you.

PSALM 89:6–8 BBE

LORD, there is no one like you! For you are great, and your name is full of power. Who would not fear you, O King of nations? That title belongs to you alone! Among all the wise people of the earth and in all the kingdoms of the world, there is no one like you.

JEREMIAH 10:6–7 NLT

"To whom will you compare me? Who is my equal?" asks the Holy One. Look up into the heavens. Who created all the stars? He brings them out one after another, calling each by its name. And he counts them to see that none are lost or have strayed away.

ISAIAH 40:25–26 NLT

Incomprehensible

"The wind blows where it wishes, and you hear the sound of it, but cannot tell where it comes from and where it goes. So is everyone who is born of the Spirit."

JOHN 3:8 NKJV

"What no eye has seen, nor ear heard, nor the human heart conceived, what God has prepared for those who love him."   1 CORINTHIANS 2:9 NRSV

"My thoughts are completely different from yours," says the LORD. "And my ways are far beyond anything you could imagine. For just as the heavens are higher than the earth, so are my ways higher than your ways and my thoughts higher than your thoughts." ISAIAH 55:8–9 NLT

No one has knowledge of the things of God.

1 CORINTHIANS 2:11 BBE

It is impossible for a limited mind to grasp the Unlimited.

Incorruptible

"You are to be perfect, even as your Father in heaven is perfect." MATTHEW 5:48 TLB

God never wants to do wrong and never tempts anyone else to do it. JAMES 1:13 TLB

Claiming to be wise, they became fools, and exchanged the glory of the immortal God for images resembling mortal man or birds or animals or reptiles. Therefore God gave them up in the lusts of their hearts to impurity. ROMANS 1:22–24 RSV

Incredible

I pray that you, . . .may have power, . . .to grasp how wide and long and high and deep is the love of Christ, and to know this love that surpasses knowledge. To him who is able to do immeasurably more than all we ask or imagine. . . EPHESIANS 3:17–20 NIV

Indispensable

"You are my Lord; apart from you I have no good thing." PSALM 16:2 NIV

Commit your work to the Lord, then it will succeed.
PROVERBS 16:3 TLB

Unless the LORD builds a house, the work of the builders is useless. Unless the LORD protects a city, guarding it with sentries will do no good. It is useless for you to work so hard from early morning until late at night, anxiously working for food to eat; for God gives rest to his loved ones.
PSALM 127:1–2 NLT

"Blessed are those who hunger and thirst for righteousness, for they will be filled."
MATTHEW 5:6 NRSV

There is nothing better for a man than taking meat and drink, and having delight in his work. This again I saw was from the hand of God. Who may take food or have pleasure without him? To the man with whom he is pleased, God gives wisdom and knowledge and joy; but to the sinner he gives the work of getting goods together and storing up wealth, to give to him in whom God has pleasure. This again is to no purpose and desire for wind.
ECCLESIASTES 2:24–26 BBE

Blessed are all who fear the LORD, who walk in his ways. You will eat the fruit of your labor; blessings and prosperity will be yours. Your wife will be like a fruitful vine within your house; your sons will be like olive shoots around your table.
PSALM 128:1–3 NIV

(Jesus taught,) "But you shouldn't be so concerned about perishable things like food. No, spend your energy seeking the eternal life that I, the Messiah, can give you. For God the Father has sent me for this very purpose."   JOHN 6:27 TLB

It is the same to me if I am looked down on or honoured; everywhere and in all things I have the secret of how to be full and how to go without food; how to have wealth and how to be in need. I am able to do all things through him who gives me strength.

PHILIPPIANS 4:12–13 BBE

Infinite
See "Everlasting."

"How great is God—beyond our understanding! The number of his years is past finding out."

JOB 36:26 NIV

Instructor
See "Counselor," "Guide," "Teacher."

"See, God is exalted in his power; who is a teacher like him?"   JOB 36:22 NRSV

"From this time forth I make you hear new things, hidden things which you have not known."

ISAIAH 48:6 RSV

Intimate

"What is the price of five sparrows? A couple of pennies? Not much more than that. Yet God does not forget a single one of them. And he knows the number of hairs on your head! Never fear, you are far more valuable to him than a whole flock of sparrows."

LUKE 12:6–7 TLB

All my hairs are numbered! How much more important is one tiny detail of my life, than one piece of hair in my head that falls out without me even noticing!

"He *(God)* will sit and judge like a refiner of silver, watching closely as the dross is burned away. He will purify *[our lives]*, refining them like gold or silver."

MALACHI 3:3 NLT

"Do not worry about your life, what you will eat or drink; or about your body, what you will wear. Is not life more important than food, and the body more important than clothes? Look at the birds of the air; they do not sow or reap or store away in barns, and yet your heavenly Father feeds them. Are you not much more valuable than they? Who of you by worrying can add a single hour to his life? And why do you worry about clothes? See how the lilies of the field grow. They do not labor or spin. Yet I tell you that not even Solomon in all his splendor was dressed like one of these. If that is how God clothes the grass of the field, which is here today and tomorrow is thrown into the fire, will he not much more clothe you?. . .Your heavenly Father knows that you need them. But seek first his kingdom and his righteousness, and all these things will be given to you."

MATTHEW 6:25–30, 32–33 NIV

"The glory that you have given me *(Jesus)* I have given them, so that they may be one, as we are one, I in them and you in me, that they may become completely one, so that the world may know that you have sent me and have loved them even as you have loved me."

JOHN 17:22–23 NRSV

But he who is united to the Lord becomes one spirit with him.   1 CORINTHIANS 6:17 RSV

"The LORD searches every heart and understands every motive behind the thoughts."   1 CHRONICLES 28:9 NIV

God is not just "out there somewhere"; He is in each of us who believes and loves Jesus.

For no one ever hates his own body, but he nourishes and tenderly cares for it, just as Christ does for the church, because we are members of his body.

EPHESIANS 5:29–30 NRSV

God shall wipe away all tears from their eyes.

REVELATION 21:4 KJV

Intolerant of sin

Your eyes are too pure to look on evil; you cannot tolerate wrong. HABAKKUK 1:13 NIV

But the Lord has made up his mind to wipe out even the memory of evil men from the earth. PSALM 34:16 TLB

For the reward of sin is death. ROMANS 6:23 BBE

But the wicked will be destroyed; they have no future.

PSALM 37:38 NLT

The Lord loathes all cheating and dishonesty.

PROVERBS 20:23 TLB

The fear of the LORD is hatred of evil. Pride and arrogance and the way of evil and perverted speech I *(the LORD)* hate.   PROVERBS 8:13 RSV

The LORD has given full vent to his wrath; he has poured out his fierce anger. He kindled a fire in Zion that consumed her foundations. The kings of the earth did not believe, nor did any of the world's people, that enemies and foes could enter the gates of Jerusalem. But it happened because of the sins of her prophets and the iniquities of her priests, who shed within her the blood of the righteous.

LAMENTATIONS 4:11–13 NIV

"But the cowardly, unbelieving, abominable, murderers, sexually immoral, sorcerers, idolaters, and all liars shall have their part in the lake which burns with fire and brimstone, which is the second death."

REVELATION 21:8 NKJV

If any man gives worship to the beast and his image, . . . To him will be given of the wine of God's wrath. . . and he will have cruel pain, burning with fire before the holy angels and before the Lamb: And the smoke of their pain goes up for ever and ever; and they have no rest day and night.   REVELATION 14:9–11 BBE

But God is love. He longs to forgive each one of us and to have a relationship with each one of us. See "Forgiving," "Yearning," "Love."

They speak of how you *(Christians)* are looking forward to the return of God's Son from heaven—Jesus, whom God brought back to life—and he is our only Savior from God's terrible anger against sin.

1THESSALONIANS 1:10 TLB

Invisible

See, I go forward, but he is not there; and back, but I do not see him; I am looking for him on the left hand, but there is no sign of him; and turning to the right, I am not able to see him. JOB 23:8–9 BBE

No one has ever seen God. It is God the only Son, who is close to the Father's heart, who has made him known.
JOHN 1:18 NRSV

"By faith—by believing God—we know that the world and the stars—in fact, all things—were made at God's command; and that they were all made from things that can't be seen. HEBREWS 11:3 TLB

By faith Moses, when he became of age, refused to be called the son of Pharaoh's daughter, choosing rather to suffer affliction with the people of God than to enjoy the passing pleasures of sin, esteeming the reproach of Christ greater riches than the treasures in Egypt; for he looked to the reward. By faith he forsook Egypt, not fearing the wrath of the king; for he endured as seeing Him who is invisible.   HEBREWS 11:24–27 NKJV

So we fix our eyes not on what is seen, but on what is unseen. For what is seen is temporary, but what is unseen is eternal.   2 CORINTHIANS 4:18 NIV

Jealous

"You shall worship no other god, for the LORD, whose name is Jealous, is a jealous God."

EXODUS 34:14 NKJV

"You must worship no other gods, but only the LORD, for he is a God who is passionate about his relationship with you."   EXODUS 34:14 NLT

"The LORD. . .is a holy and jealous God. He will not forgive your rebellion and sins. If you forsake the LORD and serve other gods, he will turn against you and destroy you, even though he has been so good to you."

JOSHUA 24:19–20 NLT

Thou shalt have no other gods before me. Thou shalt not make unto thee any graven image, or any likeness of any thing that is in heaven above, or that is in the earth beneath, or that is in the water under the earth. Thou shalt not bow down thyself to them, nor serve them: for I the LORD thy God am a jealous God, visiting the iniquity of the fathers upon the children unto the third and fourth generation of them that hate me; And shewing mercy unto thousands of them that love me, and keep my commandments.   EXODUS 20:3–6 KJV

The Lord is a jealous and avenging God; the LORD takes vengeance and is filled with wrath. The LORD takes vengeance on his foes and maintains his wrath against his enemies. The LORD is slow to anger and great in power; the LORD will not leave the guilty unpunished. His way is in the whirlwind and the storm, and clouds are the dust of his feet. . . . The earth trembles at his presence, the world and all who live in it. Who can withstand his indignation? Who can endure his fierce anger?   NAHUM 1:2–3, 5–6 NIV

God is jealous over those he loves; that is why he takes vengeance on those who hurt them. He furiously destroys their enemies. He is slow in getting angry, but when aroused, his power is incredible, and he does not easily forgive.   NAHUM 1:2–3 TLB

"We must obey God rather than men!"   ACTS 5:29 NIV

"Neither their silver nor their gold will be able to save them on the day of the LORD's wrath. In the fire of his jealousy the whole world will be consumed, for he will make a sudden end of all who live in the earth."

ZEPHANIAH 1:18 NIV

"Has the Lord as great delight in burnt offerings and sacrifices, as in obedience to the voice of the Lord? Surely, to obey is better than sacrifice, and to heed than the fat of rams." 1 SAMUEL 15:22 NRSV

Joy

Honor and majesty are before him; strength and joy are in his place. 1 CHRONICLES 16:27 RSV

Let the heavens rejoice, let the earth be glad; let them say among the nations, "The LORD reigns!" Let the sea resound, and all that is in it; let the fields be jubilant, and everything in them! Then the trees of the forest will sing, they will sing for joy before the LORD.

1 CHRONICLES 16:31–33 NIV

Oh come, let us sing to the Lord! Let us shout joyfully to the Rock of our salvation. Let us come before His presence with thanksgiving; Let us shout joyfully to Him with psalms. PSALM 95:1–2 NKJV

For the kingdom of God is not food and drink but righteousness and peace and joy in the Holy Spirit.

ROMANS 14:17 RSV

Rejoice evermore. Pray without ceasing. In every thing give thanks: for this is the will of God in Christ Jesus concerning you.   1 THESSALONIANS 5:16–18 KJV

"The joy of the Lord is your strength."

NEHEMIAH 8:10 NKJV

"Until now you have asked nothing in My name. Ask, and you will receive, that your joy may be full."

JOHN 16:24 NKJV

"All my springs are in You" *(the Lord)*.   PSALM 87:7 RSV

Judge

Here is my final conclusion: Fear God and obey his commands, for this is the duty of every person. God will judge us for everything we do, including every secret thing, whether good or bad.

ECCLESIASTES 12:13–14 NLT

"The LORD searches every heart and understands every motive behind the thoughts."   1 CHRONICLES 28:9 NIV

"For God carefully watches the way people live; he sees everything they do. No darkness is thick enough to hide the wicked from his eyes."

JOB 34:21–22 NLT

"God will judge everyone, both good and bad, for all their deeds." ECCLESIASTES 3:17 NLT

For see, the Lord will come with fire and with swift chariots of doom to pour out the fury of his anger and his hot rebuke with flames of fire. For the Lord will punish the world by fire and by his sword, and the slain of the Lord shall be many! ISAIAH 66:15–16 TLB

And I will put her children to death; and all the churches will see that I am he who makes search into the secret thoughts and hearts of men: and I will give to every one of you the reward of your works.

REVELATION 2:23 BBE

But why dost thou judge thy brother? or why dost thou set at nought thy brother? for we shall all stand before the judgment seat of Christ. For it is written, As I live, saith the Lord, every knee shall bow to me, and every tongue shall confess to God. So then every one of us shall give account of himself to God. Let us not therefore judge one another any more: but judge this rather, that no man put a stumblingblock or an occasion to fall in his brother's way. ROMANS 14:10–13 KJV

99

"And these will go away into eternal punishment, but the righteous into eternal life."   MATTHEW 25:46 NRSV

(To believers:) But if punishment does come, it is sent by the Lord, so that we may be safe when the world is judged.   1 CORINTHIANS 11: 32 BBE

Believers are disciplined while they are still here in this world. Their judgment when the Lord returns will not be the horrible punishment of the unbelievers but rewards for what they have done for the kingdom of God.

From now on there is reserved for me the crown of righteousness, which the Lord, the righteous judge, will give me on that day, and not only to me but also to all who have longed for his appearing.

2 TIMOTHY 4:8 NRSV

Just

The LORD is known for his justice. The wicked have trapped themselves in their own snares.

PSALM 9:16 NLT

"We cannot imagine the power of the Almighty, and yet he is so just and merciful that he does not destroy us."   JOB 37:23 TLB

Good and upright is the Lord.   PSALM 25:8 BBE

To do what is right and true is more pleasing to the Lord than an offering.   PROVERBS 21:3 BBE

Do no wrong in your judging: do not give thought to the position of the poor, or honour to the position of the great; but be a judge to your neighbour in righteousness.   LEVITICUS 19:15 BBE

Crooked minds are an abomination to the Lord, but those of blameless ways are his delight.   PROVERBS 11:20 NRSV

For the LORD is righteous, he loves righteous deeds; the upright shall behold his face.   PSALM 11:7 RSV

For I will proclaim the name of the Lord; ascribe greatness to our God! The Rock, his work is perfect, and all his ways are just. A faithful God, without deceit, just and upright is he.   DEUTERONOMY 32:3–4 NRSV

Justifier

And those whom he predestined he also called; and those whom he called he also justified; and those whom he justified he also glorified.   ROMANS 8:30 NRSV

101

And having chosen them, he called them to come to him. And he gave them right standing with himself, and he promised them his glory.   ROMANS 8:30 NLT

And now he has made all of this plain to us by the coming of our Savior Jesus Christ, who broke the power of death and showed us the way of everlasting life through trusting him. . . . for I know the one in whom I trust, and I am sure that he is able to safely guard all that I have given him until the day of his return.

2 TIMOTHY 1:10, 12 TLB

Kind

"I am the Lord, exercising lovingkindness, judgment, and righteousness in the earth. For in these I delight," says the Lord.   JEREMIAH 9:24 NKJV

"For the mountains shall depart And the hills be removed, But My kindness shall not depart from you, Nor shall My covenant of peace be removed," Says the Lord, who has mercy on you.   ISAIAH 54:10 NKJV

"In a surge of anger I hid my face from you for a moment, but with everlasting kindness I will have compassion on you," says the LORD your Redeemer.

ISAIAH 54:8 NIV

Or do you despise the riches of his kindness and forbearance and patience? Do you not realize that God's kindness is meant to lead you to repentance?

ROMANS 2:4 NRSV

He who oppresses the poor shows contempt for their Maker, but whoever is kind to the needy honors God.

PROVERBS 14:31 NIV

[God] raised us up with him and seated us with him in the heavenly places in Christ Jesus, so that in the ages to come he might show the immeasurable riches of his grace in kindness toward us in Christ Jesus.

EPHESIANS 2:6–7 NRSV

King of kings

Then I saw heaven opened and a white horse standing there; and the one sitting on the horse was named "Faithful and True". . . . On his robe and thigh was written this title: "King of Kings and Lord of Lords."

REVELATION 19:11,16 TLB

To the King of the ages, immortal, invisible, the only God, be honor and glory forever and ever.

1 TIMOTHY 1:17 NRSV

He who is the blessed and only Sovereign, the King of kings and Lord of lords. It is he alone who has immortality and dwells in unapproachable light, whom no one has ever seen or can see; to him be honor and eternal dominion. 1 TIMOTHY 6:15–16 NRSV

Knowledge
See "Omniscient."

"Blessed be the name of God forever and ever, for he alone has all wisdom and all power. . . . He gives wise men their wisdom and scholars their intelligence. He reveals profound mysteries beyond man's understanding. He knows all hidden things, for he is light, and darkness is no obstacle to him." DANIEL 2:20–22 TLB

"God's voice thunders in marvelous ways; he does great things beyond our understanding." JOB 37:5 NIV

Leader
See "God of gods," "King of kings," "Lord of lords."

"For the Lord your God is God of gods and Lord of lords, the great God, mighty and awesome, who shows no partiality nor takes a bribe."

DEUTERONOMY 10:17 NKJV

Life

My son, attend to my words; incline thine ear unto my sayings. Let them not depart from thine eyes; keep them in the midst of thine heart. For they are life unto those that find them, and health to all their flesh.

PROVERBS 4:20–22 KJV

One does not live by bread alone, but by every word that comes from the mouth of the Lord.

DEUTERONOMY 8:3 NRSV

Food isn't everything, . . .real life comes by obeying every command of God.　　DEUTERONOMY 8:3 TLB

Follow my advice, my son; always keep it in mind and stick to it. Obey me and live! Guard my words as your most precious possession.　　PROVERBS 7:1–2 TLB

The fear of the Lord *(to hate evil, Proverbs 8:13)* is a fountain of life, by which one may be turned from the nets of death.　　PROVERBS 14:27 BBE

The fear of the LORD is the beginning of wisdom, and the knowledge of the Holy One is insight. For by me your days will be multiplied, and years will be added to your life.　　PROVERBS 9:10–11 NRSV

God, the giver of life, . . .   1 TIMOTHY 6:13 BBE

God. . .who gives life to the dead and calls into existence the things that do not exist. . .   ROMANS 4:17 RSV

We must all die; we are like water spilled on the ground, which cannot be gathered up. But God will not take away a life; he will devise plans so as not to keep an outcast banished forever from his presence.

2 SAMUEL 14:14 NRSV

"I have come that they may have life, and that they may have it more abundantly."   JOHN 10:10 NKJV

Light

God is light and in him there is nothing dark.

1 JOHN 1:5 BBE

O Lord, you are my light! You make my darkness bright.   2 SAMUEL 22:29 TLB

The Lord is my light and my salvation.

PSALM 27:1 NKJV

Your words are a flashlight to light the path ahead of me, and keep me from stumbling.   PSALM 119:105 TLB

(Jesus said,) "I am the light of the world."

JOHN 9:5 RSV

Once you were darkness, but now you are light in the Lord; walk as children of light (for the fruit of light is found in all that is good and right and true).

EPHESIANS 5:8–9 RSV

Violence will disappear out of your land—all war will end. Your walls will be "Salvation" and your gates "Praise." No longer will you need the sun or moon to give you light, for the Lord your God will be your ever-lasting light, and he will be your glory. Your sun shall never set; the moon shall not go down—for the Lord will be your everlasting light; your days of mourning all will end.

ISAIAH 60:18–20 TLB

Every good and true thing is given to us from heaven, coming from the Father of lights, with whom there is no change or any shade made by turning.

JAMES 1:17 BBE

Living

But the Lord is the true God; He is the living God and the everlasting King. At His wrath the earth will tremble, And the nations will not be able to endure His indignation.

JEREMIAH 10:10 NKJV

"For he is the living God, and he will endure forever. His kingdom will never be destroyed, and his rule will never end."

DANIEL 6:26 NLT

"You should turn from these useless things to the living God, who made the heaven, the earth, the sea, and all things that are in them."

ACTS 14:15 NKJV

"What have you gained by worshiping all your manmade idols? How foolish to trust in something made by your own hands! What fools you are to believe such lies! How terrible it will be for you who beg lifeless wooden idols to save you. You ask speechless stone images to tell you what to do. Can an idol speak for God? They may be overlaid with gold and silver, but they are lifeless inside. But the LORD is in his holy Temple. Let all the earth be silent before him."

HABAKKUK 2:18–20 NLT

When men tell you to consult mediums and spiritists, who whisper and mutter, should not a people inquire of their God? Why consult the dead on behalf of the living?

ISAIAH 8:19 NIV

As a deer longs for flowing streams, so my soul longs for you, O God. My soul thirsts for God, for the living God. When shall I come and behold the face of God?

PSALM 42:1–2 NRSV

Lofty
See "Transcendent."

The High and Lofty One Who inhabits eternity. . .
ISAIAH 57:15 NKJV

Lord of lords

For the LORD is the great God, the great King above all gods. In his hand are the depths of the earth, and the mountain peaks belong to him. The sea is his, for he made it, and his hands formed the dry land. Come, let us bow down in worship, let us kneel before the LORD our Maker.
PSALM 95:3–6 NIV

For the Lord your God is God of gods and Lord of lords, the great God, strong in power and greatly to be feared, who has no respect for any man's position and takes no rewards.
DEUTERONOMY 10:17 BBE

Love

Greater love has no man than this, that a man gives up his life for his friends.
JOHN 15:13 BBE

We love because he first loved us.
1 JOHN 4:19 NRSV

But anyone who does not love does not know God—for God is love. God showed how much he loved us by sending his only Son into the world so that we might have eternal life through him. This is real love. It is not that we loved God, but that he loved us and sent his Son as a sacrifice to take away our sins.

1 JOHN 4:8–10 NLT

God showed how much he loved us by sending his only Son into this wicked world to bring to us eternal life through his death. 1 JOHN 4:9 TLB

For as the heavens are high above the earth, so great is his steadfast love toward those who fear him.

PSALM 103:11 RSV

For your steadfast love is higher than the heavens, and your faithfulness reaches to the clouds.

PSALM 108:4 NRSV

But if a person isn't loving and kind, it shows that he doesn't know God—for God is love. 1 JOHN 4:8 TLB

There is no fear in love. But perfect love *(which is God)* drives out fear. 1 JOHN 4:18 NIV

The LORD, your God, . . .will rejoice over you with gladness, he will renew you in his love; he will exult over you with loud singing. ZEPHANIAH 3:17 RSV

Love is patient, love is kind. It does not envy, it does not boast, it is not proud. It is not rude, it is not self-seeking, it is not easily angered, it keeps no record of wrongs. Love does not delight in evil but rejoices with the truth. It always protects, always trusts, always hopes, always perseveres. Love never fails.

1 CORINTHIANS 13:4–8 NIV

Loyal

For I am convinced that neither death, nor life, nor angels, nor rulers, nor things present, nor things to come, nor powers, nor height, nor depth, nor anything else in all creation, will be able to separate us from the love of God in Christ Jesus our Lord.

ROMANS 8:38–39 NRSV

God is like the father in the story of the prodigal son. The son asked the father for his inheritance, took it, and left for a distant land. The father loved his son and longed for him to return. The son, in the meantime, squandered all his inheritance in wild and foolish living and became destitute. The son, in desperation, decided to humbly return to the father. The father did not disown the son for his foolish actions. Instead, the father was so happy at the son's return, that without even needing to have the son demonstrate a change of heart, the father immediately invited everyone to celebrate and to share his happiness with him.

111

And his son said to him, Father, I have done wrong, against heaven and in your eyes: I am no longer good enough to be named your son. But the father said to his servants, Get out the first robe quickly, and put it on him, and put a ring on his hand and shoes on his feet: And get the fat young ox and put it to death, and let us have a feast, and be glad. For this, my son, who was dead, is living again; he had gone away from me, and has come back. And they were full of joy.

LUKE 15:21–24 BBE

I sought the Lord, and He heard me, And delivered me from all my fears. PSALM 34:4 NKJV

"I love those who love me, and those who seek me find me. With me are riches and honor, enduring wealth and prosperity. My fruit is better than fine gold; what I yield surpasses choice silver. I walk in the way of righteousness, along the paths of justice, bestowing wealth on those who love me and making their treasuries full." PROVERBS 8:17–21 NIV

"Because he loves me," says the LORD, "I will rescue him; I will protect him, for he acknowledges my name. He will call upon me, and I will answer him; I will be with him in trouble, I will deliver him and honor him. With long life will I satisfy him and show him my salvation." PSALM 91:14–16 NIV

Then those who feared the Lord spoke to one another, and the Lord listened and heard them; So a book of remembrance was written before Him for those who fear the Lord and who meditate on His name. "They shall be Mine," says the LORD of hosts, "On the day that I make them My jewels. And I will spare them as a man spares his own son who serves him."

MALACHI 3:16–17 NKJV

Majestic

Bless the LORD, O my soul. O LORD my God, thou art very great; thou art clothed with honour and majesty. Who coverest thyself with light as with a garment: who stretchest out the heavens like a curtain: Who layeth the beams of his chambers in the waters: who maketh the clouds his chariot: who walketh upon the wings of the wind: Who maketh his angels spirits; his ministers a flaming fire.

PSALM 104:1–4 KJV

The LORD reigneth, he is clothed with majesty; the LORD is clothed with strength, wherewith he hath girded himself: the world also is stablished, that it cannot be moved. Thy throne is established of old: thou art from everlasting. The floods have lifted up, O LORD, the floods have lifted up their voice; the floods lift up their waves. The LORD on high is mightier than the noise of many waters, yea, than the mighty waves of the sea. Thy testimonies are very sure: holiness becometh thine house, O LORD, for ever.   PSALM 93:1–5 KJV

Glorious are you, more majestic than the everlasting mountains.   PSALM 76:4 NRSV

Marvelous

"God thunders marvelously with His voice; He does great things which we cannot comprehend."

JOB 37:5 NKJV

Blessed be the Lord, the God of Israel, who alone does wondrous things. Blessed be his glorious name forever; may his glory fill the whole earth.

PSALM 72:18–19 NRSV

"Great and marvelous are your deeds, Lord God Almighty. Just and true are your ways, King of the ages. Who will not fear you, O Lord, and bring glory to your name? For you alone are holy. All nations will come and worship before you."   REVELATION 15:3–4 NIV

Merciful

The steadfast love of the Lord never ceases, his mercies never come to an end; they are new every morning; great is your faithfulness.

LAMENTATIONS 3:22–23 NRSV

For You, Lord, are good, and ready to forgive, And abundant in mercy to all those who call upon You.

PSALM 86:5 NKJV

The LORD is merciful and gracious, slow to anger, and plenteous in mercy. He will not always chide: neither will he keep his anger for ever. He hath not dealt with us after our sins; nor rewarded us according to our iniquities. For as the heaven is high above the earth, so great is his mercy toward them that fear him. As far as the east is from the west, so far hath he removed our transgressions from us. Like as a father pitieth his children, so the LORD pitieth them that fear him. For he knoweth our frame; he remembereth that we are dust. As for man, his days are as grass: as a flower of the field, so he flourisheth. For the wind passeth over it, and it is gone; and the place thereof shall know it no more. But the mercy of the LORD is from everlasting to everlasting upon them that fear him, and his righteousness unto children's children; To such as keep his covenant, and to those that remember his commandments to do them.   PSALM 103:8–18 KJV

The Lord is so full of mercy that He disapproves when we ourselves are not merciful.

Because my desire is for mercy and not offerings; for the knowledge of God more than for burned offerings.

HOSEA 6:6 BBE

Do not rejoice when your enemies fall, and do not let your heart be glad when they stumble, or else the Lord will see it and be displeased, and turn away his anger from them.   PROVERBS 24:17–18 NRSV

I want you to be merciful; I don't want your sacrifices. I want you to know God; that's more important than burnt offerings.   HOSEA 6:6 NLT

" 'I will frown on you no longer, for I am merciful,' declares the LORD, 'I will not be angry forever. Only acknowledge your guilt—you have rebelled against the LORD your God, you have scattered your favors. . . and have not obeyed me,' " declares the LORD.

JEREMIAH 3:12–13 NIV

He who keeps his sins secret will not do well; but one who is open about them, and gives them up, will get mercy.   PROVERBS 28:13 BBE

Let the wicked forsake his way, and the unrighteous man his thoughts: and let him return unto the LORD, and he will have mercy upon him; and to our God, for he will abundantly pardon. For my thoughts are not your thoughts, neither are your ways my ways, saith the LORD. For as the heavens are higher than the earth, so are my ways higher than your ways, and my thoughts than your thoughts.   ISAIAH 55:7–9 KJV

We are not offering our prayers before you because of our righteousness, but because of your great mercies.
                                                    DANIEL 9:18 BBE

He *(God)* saved us, not because of righteous things we had done, but because of his mercy.   TITUS 3:5 NIV

Mighty

O Lord God of hosts, who is as mighty as you, O Lord? Your faithfulness surrounds you. You rule the raging of the sea; when its waves rise, you still them. You crushed Rahab like a carcass; you scattered your enemies with your mighty arm. The heavens are yours, the earth also is yours; the world and all that is in it— you have founded them. The north and the south—you created them; Tabor and Hermon joyously praise your name. You have a mighty arm; strong is your hand, high your right hand. Righteousness and justice are the foundation of your throne; steadfast love and faithfulness go before you.   PSALM 89:8–14 NRSV

"The Mighty One, God, the LORD!"   JOSHUA 22:22 NIV

He sees the number of the stars; he gives them all their names. Great is our Lord, and great his power; there is no limit to his wisdom.   PSALM 147:4–5 BBE

"With Him are wisdom and strength, He has counsel and understanding. If He breaks a thing down, it cannot be rebuilt; If He imprisons a man, there can be no release. If He withholds the waters, they dry up; If He sends them out, they overwhelm the earth."

JOB 12:13–15 NKJV

"The Lord your God in your midst, The Mighty One, will save; He will rejoice over you with gladness, He will quiet you in His love, He will rejoice over you with singing."   ZEPHANIAH 3:17 NKJV

Miraculous

You are the God who performs miracles.

PSALM 77:14 NIV

(God) Who does great things outside our knowledge, wonders without number: Who gives rain on the earth, and sends water on the fields: Lifting up those who are low, and putting the sad in a safe place; Who makes the designs of the wise go wrong, so that they are unable to give effect to their purposes.   JOB 5:9–12 BBE

And they forgot about the wonderful miracles God had done for them, and for their fathers in Egypt. For he divided the sea before them and led them through! The water stood banked up along both sides of them! In the daytime he led them by a cloud, and at night by a pillar of fire. He split open the rocks in the wilderness to give them plenty of water, as though gushing from a spring. Streams poured from the rock, flowing like a river!   PSALM 78:11–16 TLB

God of gods! . . . Lord of lords! . . . To Him who alone does great wonders. . .   PSALM 136:2–4 NKJV

The God. . .who gives life to the dead and calls into existence the things that do not exist. . .

ROMANS 4:17 RSV

Most High

It is my pleasure to tell you about the miraculous signs and wonders that the Most High God has performed for me. How great are his signs, how mighty his wonders!   DANIEL 4:2–3 NIV

" 'The Most High is sovereign over the kingdom of mortals; he gives it to whom he will and sets over it the lowliest of human beings.' "   DANIEL 4:17 NRSV

You, whose name alone is the Lord, Are the Most High over all the earth. PSALM 83:18 NKJV

"Yet the Most High does not dwell in houses made with human hands; as the prophet says, 'Heaven is my throne, and the earth is my footstool. What kind of house will you build for me, says the Lord, or what is the place of my rest? Did not my hand make all these things?' " ACTS 7:48–50 NRSV

Near

But you are near, O Lord; all your commandments are based on truth. PSALM 119:151 TLB

The LORD is near to all who call upon him, to all who call upon him in truth. PSALM 145:18 RSV

Seek the Lord while He may be found, Call upon Him while He is near. ISAIAH 55:6 NKJV

We thank you, O God! We give thanks because you are near. People everywhere tell of your mighty miracles. PSALM 75:1 NLT

Come near to God and he will come near to you. JAMES 4:8 BBE

The LORD is faithful to all his promises and loving toward all he has made. The LORD upholds all those who fall and lifts up all who are bowed down. The eyes of all look to you, and you give them their food at the proper time. You open your hand and satisfy the desires of every living thing. The LORD is righteous in all his ways and loving toward all he has made. The LORD is near to all who call on him, to all who call on him in truth. He fulfills the desires of those who fear him; he hears their cry and saves them. The LORD watches over all who love him, but all the wicked he will destroy. PSALM 145:13–20 NIV

"Look, the virgin shall conceive and bear a son, and they shall name him Emmanuel," which means, "God is with us." MATTHEW 1:23 NRSV

Nurturing

He will feed his flock like a shepherd. He will carry the lambs in his arms, holding them close to his heart. He will gently lead the mother sheep with their young.

ISAIAH 40:11 NLT

"For the eyes of the Lord run to and fro throughout the whole earth, to show Himself strong on behalf of those whose heart is loyal to Him." 2 CHRONICLES 16:9 NKJV

" 'For this is what the Sovereign LORD says: I myself will search for my sheep and look after them. As a shepherd looks after his scattered flock when he is with them, so will I look after my sheep. I will rescue them from all the places where they were scattered on a day of clouds and darkness. . .I will bring them into their own land. . .I will tend them in a good pasture. . . . There they will lie down in good grazing land, and there they will feed in a rich pasture. . . . I myself will tend my sheep and have them lie down, declares the Sovereign LORD. I will search for the lost and bring back the strays. I will bind up the injured and strengthen the weak, . . . I will shepherd the flock with justice.' " EZEKIEL 34:11–16 NIV

Let nothing be done through selfish ambition or conceit, but in lowliness of mind let each esteem others better than himself. PHILIPPIANS 2:3 NKJV

Consider that God Himself, in spite of His immeasurable superiority in all areas, does nothing out of selfish ambition or vain conceit but out of care and compassion for us.

"The Almighty is beyond our reach and exalted in power; in his justice and great righteousness, he does not oppress." JOB 37:23 NIV

Be devoted to one another in brotherly love. Honor one another above yourselves. ROMANS 12:10 NIV

For the Lord will comfort Zion, He will comfort all her waste places; He will make her wilderness like Eden, and her desert like the garden of the Lord; Joy and gladness will be found in it, Thanksgiving and the voice of melody.

ISAIAH 51:3 NKJV

Since we, God's children, are human beings—made of flesh and blood—he became flesh and blood too by being born in human form; for only as a human being could he die and in dying break the power of the devil who had the power of death. Only in that way could he deliver those who through fear of death have been living all their lives as slaves to constant dread.

HEBREWS 2:14–15 TLB

Omnipotent
All powerful; limitless power.

For there is nothing which God is not able to do.

LUKE 1:37 BBE

It is he *(God)* who made the earth by his power, who established the world by his wisdom, and by his understanding stretched out the heavens.

JEREMIAH 10:12 RSV

"But he is unchangeable and who can turn him? What he desires, that he does."

JOB 23:13 RSV

"For assuredly, I say to you, till heaven and earth pass away, one jot or one tittle will by no means pass from the law till all is fulfilled." MATTHEW 5:18 NKJV

A "jot" is like the dot of an "i," and a "tittle" is the smallest mark that can be made in a word or letter. Imagine that the smallest fraction of one letter in God's law is more reliable and dependable than all of heaven and earth!

Many are the plans in the mind of a man, but it is the purpose of the LORD that will be established.
PROVERBS 19:21 RSV

No wisdom, no understanding, no counsel, can avail against the LORD. PROVERBS 21:30 RSV

"I know that you can do anything and that no one can stop you." JOB 42:2 TLB

(God declares,) "When I act, who can reverse it?"
ISAIAH 43:13 NIV

And I say to you, my friends, Have no fear of those who may put the body to death, and are able to do no more than that. But I will make clear to you of whom you are to be in fear: of him who after death has power to send you to hell; yes, truly I say, Have fear of him.
LUKE 12:4–5 BBE

A man can do nothing better than to eat and drink and find satisfaction in his work. This too, I see, is from the hand of God, for without him, who can eat or find enjoyment? To the man who pleases him, God gives wisdom, knowledge and happiness, but to the sinner he gives the task of gathering and storing up wealth to hand it over to the one who pleases God.

ECCLESIASTES 2:24–26 NIV

God is incomprehensibly far above us in power and wisdom. He is so powerful that He will accomplish His purpose in this world while still giving us the complete freedom to choose and to do whatever we want!

Do not call conspiracy all that this people calls conspiracy, and do not fear what it fears, or be in dread. But the Lord of hosts, him you shall regard as holy; let him be your fear, and let him be your dread.

ISAIAH 8:12–13 NRSV

"With God are wisdom and might; he has counsel and understanding. If he tears down, none can rebuild; if he shuts a man in, none can open. If he withholds the waters, they dry up; if he sends them out, they overwhelm the land." JOB 12:13–15 RSV

The fear of man brings a snare, But whoever trusts in the Lord shall be safe. PROVERBS 29:25 NKJV

Men will flee to caves in the rocks and to holes in the ground from dread of the LORD and the splendor of his majesty, when he rises to shake the earth. In that day men will throw away to the rodents and bats their idols of silver and idols of gold, which they made to worship. They will flee to caverns in the rocks and to the overhanging crags from dread of the LORD and the splendor of his majesty, when he rises to shake the earth. Stop trusting in man, who has but a breath in his nostrils.   ISAIAH 2:19–22 NIV

"What he opens no one can shut, and what he shuts no one can open."   REVELATION 3:7 NIV

Omnipresent
Is everywhere, including here.

For of him, and through him, and to him, are all things.   ROMANS 11:36 BBE

One God and Father of all, who is over all, and through all, and in all.   EPHESIANS 4:6 BBE

"The LORD is there."   EZEKIEL 48:35 RSV

The Lord is God, in heaven on high and here on earth; there is no other God.   DEUTERONOMY 4:39 BBE

The eyes of the LORD are in every place, keeping watch on the evil and the good.   PROVERBS 15:3 RSV

Where may I go from your spirit? how may I go in flight from you? If I go up to heaven, you are there: or if I make my bed in the underworld, you are there. If I take the wings of the morning, and go to the farthest parts of the sea; Even there will I be guided by your hand, and your right hand will keep me.

PSALM 139:7–10 BBE

"Am I a God who is only in one place and cannot see what they are doing? Can anyone hide from me? Am I not everywhere in all of heaven and earth?"

JEREMIAH 23:23–24 TLB

Omniscient
Knows all things.

By wisdom the LORD founded the earth; by understanding he established the heavens. By his knowledge the deep fountains of the earth burst forth, and the clouds poured down rain.   PROVERBS 3:19–20 NLT

For God's foolishness is wiser than human wisdom.

1 CORINTHIANS 1:25 NRSV

"Even from the beginning I have declared it to you;
Before it came to pass I proclaimed it to you, Lest you
should say, 'My idol has done them, And my carved
image and my molded image Have commanded them.'
You have heard; See all this. And will you not declare
it? I have made you hear new things from this time,
Even hidden things, and you did not know them."

ISAIAH 48:5–6 NKJV

He knows about everyone, everywhere. Everything
about us is bare and wide open to the all-seeing eyes
of our living God; nothing can be hidden from him to
whom we must explain all that we have done.

HEBREWS 4:13 TLB

You have put our evil doings before you, our secret
sins in the light of your face.   PSALM 90:8 BBE

For God is closely watching you, and he weighs carefully everything you do.   PROVERBS 5:21 TLB

Then she called the name of the Lord who spoke to
her, You-Are-the-God-Who-Sees. GENESIS 16:13 NKJV

From heaven the LORD looks down and sees all
mankind; from his dwelling place he watches all who
live on earth—he who forms the hearts of all, who con-
siders everything they do.   PSALM 33:13–15 NIV

"For there is nothing covered that will not be revealed, nor hidden that will not be known. Therefore whatever you have spoken in the dark will be heard in the light, and what you have spoken in the ear in inner rooms will be proclaimed on the housetops."

LUKE 12:2–3 NKJV

"Blessed be the name of God forever and ever, for he alone has all wisdom and all power. World events are under his control. He removes kings and sets others on their thrones. He gives wise men their wisdom and scholars their intelligence. He reveals profound mysteries beyond man's understanding. He knows all hidden things, for he is light, and darkness is no obstacle to him."

DANIEL 2:20–22 TLB

One God

You believe that there is one God. You do well. Even the demons believe—and tremble! JAMES 2:19 NKJV

There is only one God. EPHESIANS 4:6 NLT

Organized

God is completely organized while simultaneously being incredibly creative. He created in an organized and orderly fashion everything after its own kind, but He added a randomizing factor that gave everyone and everything its very own uniqueness.

Then God said, "Let the earth bring forth the living creature according to its kind: cattle and creeping thing and beast of the earth, each according to its kind."

GENESIS 1:24 NKJV

The stork knows the time of her migration, as do the turtledove, the swallow, and the crane. They all return at the proper time each year. JEREMIAH 8:7 NLT

For God is not a God of disorder but of peace.

1 CORINTHIANS 14:33 NIV

Over All

"Indeed heaven and the highest heavens belong to the Lord your God, also the earth with all that is in it."

DEUTERONOMY 10:14 NKJV

One God and Father of all, who is above all and through all and in all. . . EPHESIANS 4:6 NRSV

Overcomer
See "Victorious."

The LORD is my banner. EXODUS 17:15 RSV

In various traditions, a banner was flown over the winning side. God is the reason why His people are victorious; He leads all those who follow Him in triumph.

You give me your shield of victory, and your right hand sustains me; you stoop down to make me great.
PSALM 18:35 NIV

For they did not gain possession of the land by their own sword, Nor did their own arm save them; But it was Your right hand, Your arm, and the light of Your countenance, because You favored them.
PSALM 44:3 NKJV

Overwhelming

His body was like beryl, his face like lightning, his eyes like flaming torches, his arms and legs like the gleam of burnished bronze, and the sound of his words like the roar of a multitude. . . . My strength left me, and my complexion grew deathly pale, and I retained no strength. DANIEL 10:6, 8 NRSV

His head and his hair were white as white wool, white as snow; his eyes were like a flame of fire, his feet were like burnished bronze, refined as in a furnace, and his voice was like the sound of many waters; in his right hand he held seven stars, from his mouth issued a sharp two-edged sword, and his face was like the sun shining in full strength. When I saw him, I fell at his feet as though dead.   REVELATION 1:14–17 RSV

My flesh trembles for fear of you, and I am afraid of your judgments.   PSALM 119:120 NRSV

But the LORD is the true God; He is the living God and the everlasting King. At His wrath the earth will tremble, And the nations will not be able to endure His indignation.   JEREMIAH 10:10 NKJV

The mountains quake before him, the hills melt; the earth is laid waste before him, the world and all that dwell therein. Who can stand before his indignation? Who can endure the heat of his anger? His wrath is poured out like fire, and the rocks are broken asunder by him. The LORD is good, a stronghold in the day of trouble; he knows those who take refuge in him. But with an overflowing flood he will make a full end of his adversaries, and will pursue his enemies into darkness.

NAHUM 1:5–8 RSV

Passionate

"If you had responded to my rebuke, I would have poured out my heart to you and made my thoughts known to you."   PROVERBS 1:23 NIV

The LORD was grieved that he had made man on the earth, and his heart was filled with pain.

GENESIS 6:6 NIV

" 'This is what the LORD, the God of Israel, says: I will make your weapons useless. . .Yes, I will bring your enemies right into the heart of this city. I myself will fight against you with great power, for I am very angry. You have made me furious!' "   JEREMIAH 21:4–5 NLT

Behold, the day of the LORD comes, cruel, with wrath and fierce anger, to make the earth a desolation and to destroy its sinners from it. For the stars of the heavens and their constellations will not give their light; the sun will be dark at its rising and the moon will not shed its light. I will punish the world for its evil, and the wicked for their iniquity; I will put an end to the pride of the arrogant, and lay low the haughtiness of the ruthless. I will make men more rare than fine gold, and mankind than the gold of Ophir. Therefore I will make the heavens tremble, and the earth will be shaken out of its place, at the wrath of the LORD of hosts in the day of his fierce anger.   ISAIAH 13:9–13 RSV

When we treat others unkindly or selfishly or with any bad intent, God does not take it lightly; in fact, He feels so passionately about it that He takes it personally.

God has called us to be holy, not to live impure lives. Anyone who refuses to live by these rules is not disobeying human rules but is rejecting God, who gives his Holy Spirit to you.　　1 THESSALONIANS 4:7–8 NLT

The whole assembly talked about stoning them *(Moses, Aaron, Joshua and Caleb). . . .* The LORD said to Moses, "How long will these people treat me with contempt?"　　NUMBERS 14:10–11 NIV

The Lord is compassionate and gracious, . . . For as high as the heavens are above the earth, so great is his love for those who fear him.　　PSALM 103:8, 11 NIV

"Can a woman forget her nursing child, And not have compassion on the son of her womb? Surely they may forget, Yet I will not forget you."　　ISAIAH 49:15 NKJV

God loved the people of this world so much *(so passionately)* that he gave his only Son, so that everyone who has faith in him will have eternal life and never really die.　　JOHN 3:16 CEV

When the Lord saw her, his heart overflowed with compassion. "Don't cry!" he said.　　LUKE 7:13 NLT

The LORD, your God, is in your midst, a warrior who gives victory; he will rejoice over you with gladness, he will renew you in his love; he will exult over you with loud singing as on a day of festival.

ZEPHANIAH 3:17–18 RSV

Come and see the works of God; He is awesome in His doing toward the sons of men.   PSALM 66:5 NKJV

"This is what the Sovereign LORD says:. . .I will be zealous for my holy name."   EZEKIEL 39:25 NIV

Patient

" 'The LORD is slow to anger, and abounding in steadfast love, forgiving iniquity and transgression.' "

NUMBERS 14:18 RSV

"I am the LORD, I am the LORD, the merciful and gracious God. I am slow to anger and rich in unfailing love and faithfulness. I show this unfailing love to many thousands by forgiving every kind of sin and rebellion. Even so I do not leave sin unpunished, but I punish the children for the sins of their parents to the third and fourth generations."   EXODUS 34:6–7 NLT

The Lord is slow to get angry and great in power.

NAHUM 1:3 BBE

It is better to be slow-tempered than famous; it is better to have self-control than to control an army.

PROVERBS 16:32 TLB

The Lord is not slow about his promise, as some think of slowness, but is patient with you, not wanting any to perish, but all to come to repentance. 2 PETER 3:9 NRSV

Do you despise the riches of his kindness and forbearance and patience? Do you not realize that God's kindness is meant to lead you to repentance?

ROMANS 2:4 NRSV

You have no reason, whoever you are, for judging: for in judging another you are judging yourself, for you do the same things. And we are conscious that God is a true judge against those who do such things. But you who are judging another for doing what you do yourself, are you hoping that God's decision will not take effect against you? Or is it nothing to you that God had pity on you, waiting and putting up with you for so long, not seeing that in his pity God's desire is to give you a change of heart? ROMANS 2:1–4 BBE

Peace

Those who love your laws have great peace of heart and mind and do not stumble. PSALM 119:165 TLB

The LORD is peace.   JUDGES 6:24 RSV

Be anxious for nothing, but in everything by prayer and supplication, with thanksgiving, let your requests be made known to God; and the peace of God, which surpasses all understanding, will guard your hearts and minds through Christ Jesus.   PHILIPPIANS 4:6–7 NKJV

"Blessed are the peacemakers, for they shall be called sons of God."   MATTHEW 5:9 RSV

"I am the LORD your God, who teaches you what is good and leads you along the paths you should follow. Oh, that you had listened to my commands! Then you would have had peace flowing like a gentle river and righteousness rolling like waves."

ISAIAH 48:17–18 NLT

Seek peace, and pursue it.   PSALM 34:14 RSV

His name will be called "Wonderful Counselor, Mighty God, Everlasting Father, Prince of Peace." Of the increase of his government and of peace there will be no end.   ISAIAH 9:6–7 RSV

May the God of peace be with you all.

ROMANS 15:33 BBE

137

Perfect

What a God he is! How perfect in every way! All his promises prove true.　　　PSALM 18:30 TLB

"Every word of God is flawless; he is a shield to those who take refuge in him."　　　PROVERBS 30:5 NIV

Perfect love casts out fear.　　　1 JOHN 4:18 RSV

The law of the LORD is perfect, reviving the soul. The decrees of the LORD are trustworthy, making wise the simple.　　　PSALM 19:7 NLT

Out of Zion, the perfection of beauty, God will shine forth.　　　PSALM 50:2 NKJV

I will proclaim the name of the Lord; ascribe greatness to our God! The Rock, his work is perfect, and all his ways are just. A faithful God, without deceit, just and upright is he.　　　DEUTERONOMY 32:3–4 NRSV

I know that whatever God does endures for ever; nothing can be added to it, nor anything taken from it.
　　　ECCLESIASTES 3:14 RSV

"God is my strength and power, And He makes my way perfect."　　　2 SAMUEL 22:33 NKJV

"Be perfect, therefore, as your heavenly Father is perfect."

MATTHEW 5:48 NRSV

God's will is. . .good, pleasing, and perfect.

ROMANS 12:2 NIV

Persevering

The Lord isn't really being slow about his promise to return, as some people think. No, he is being patient for your sake. He does not want anyone to perish, so he is giving more time for everyone to repent.

2 PETER 3:9 NLT

Personal

Even so it is not the will of your Father which is in heaven, that one of these little ones should perish.

MATTHEW 18:14 KJV

"Can a mother forget the baby at her breast and have no compassion on the child she has borne? Though she may forget, I will not forget you! See, I have engraved you on the palms of my hands."

ISAIAH 49:15–16 NIV

Have no fear, for I have taken up your cause; naming you by your name. ISAIAH 43:1 BBE

Even the hairs of your head are numbered.

LUKE 12:7 BBE

The person who knows God cannot help but to love Him because of His personal interest and involvement with that individual.

I will praise You, O Lord my God, with all my heart, And I will glorify Your name forevermore. For great is Your mercy toward me, And You have delivered my soul from the depths of Sheol. PSALM 86:12–13 NKJV

O Lord, You have pleaded the case for my soul; You have redeemed my life. LAMENTATIONS 3:58 NKJV

Powerful

Fire goes before him, and consumes his adversaries on every side. His lightnings light up the world; the earth sees and trembles. The mountains melt like wax before the Lord. PSALM 97:3–5 NRSV

God's weakness is stronger than human strength.

1 CORINTHIANS 1:25 NRSV

For, behold, the LORD cometh forth out of his place, and will come down, and tread upon the high places of the earth. And the mountains shall be molten under him, and the valleys shall be cleft, as wax before the fire, and as the waters that are poured down a steep place.

MICAH 1:3–4 KJV

" 'Not by might nor by power, but by My Spirit,' says the Lord of hosts."   ZECHARIAH 4:6 NKJV

The Lord is slow to get angry and great in power, and will not let the sinner go without punishment: the way of the Lord is in the wind and the storm, and the clouds are the dust of his feet. He says sharp words to the sea and makes it dry, drying up all the rivers: Bashan is feeble, and Carmel, and the flower of Lebanon is without strength. The mountains are shaking because of him, and the hills flowing away; the earth is falling to bits before him, the world and all who are in it. Who may keep his place before his wrath? and who may undergo the heat of his passion? his wrath is let loose like fire and the rocks are broken open by him.

NAHUM 1:3–6 BBE

"God is not a man, that he should lie, nor a son of man, that he should change his mind. Does he speak and then not act? Does he promise and not fulfill? I have received a command to bless; he has blessed, and I cannot change it."   NUMBERS 23:19–20 NIV

The brightness was like the sun; rays came forth from his hand, where his power lay hidden.

HABAKKUK 3:4 NRSV

LORD, there is no one like you! For you are great, and your name is full of power.　　JEREMIAH 10:6 NLT

Precious

The law of the LORD is perfect, converting the soul: the testimony of the LORD is sure, making wise the simple. The statutes of the LORD are right, rejoicing the heart: the commandment of the LORD is pure, enlightening the eyes. The fear of the LORD is clean, enduring for ever: the judgments of the LORD are true and righteous altogether.

More to be desired are they than gold, yea, than much fine gold: sweeter also than honey and the honeycomb. Moreover by them is thy servant warned: and in keeping of them there is great reward.

PSALM 19:7–11 KJV

Take my instruction instead of silver, and knowledge rather than choice gold; for wisdom is better than jewels, and all that you may desire cannot compare with her.　　PROVERBS 8:10–11 RSV

Happy is the man that findeth wisdom, and the man that getteth understanding. For the merchandise of it is better than the merchandise of silver, and the gain thereof than fine gold. She is more precious than rubies: and all the things thou canst desire are not to be compared unto her. Length of days is in her right hand; and in her left hand riches and honour. Her ways are ways of pleasantness, and all her paths are peace. She is a tree of life to them that lay hold upon her: and happy is every one that retaineth her.   PROVERBS 3:13–18 KJV

My son, if you will take my words to your heart, storing up my laws in your mind; So that your ear gives attention to wisdom, and your heart is turned to knowledge; Truly, if you are crying out for good sense, and your request is for knowledge; If you are looking for her as for silver, and searching for her as for stored-up wealth; Then the fear of the Lord will be clear to you, and knowledge of God will be yours. For the Lord gives wisdom; out of his mouth come knowledge and reason.   PROVERBS 2:1–6 BBE

As we know Jesus better, his divine power gives us everything we need for living a godly life. He has called us to receive his own glory and goodness! And by that same mighty power, he has given us all of his rich and wonderful promises. He has promised that you will escape the decadence all around you caused by evil desires and that you will share in his divine nature.

2 PETER 1:3–4 NLT

How precious also are Your thoughts to me, O God! How great is the sum of them!   PSALM 139:17 NKJV

Profitable

For bodily exercise profits a little, but godliness is profitable for all things, having promise of the life that now is and of that which is to come.

1 TIMOTHY 4:8 NKJV

Protector

The name of the Lord is a strong tower; the righteous run to it and are safe.   PROVERBS 18:10 NKJV

When I cry out to You, Then my enemies will turn back; This I know, because God is for me.

PSALM 56:9 NKJV

Happy is he whose resting-place is in the secret of the Lord, and under the shade of the wings of the Most High; Who says of the Lord, He is my safe place and my tower of strength: he is my God, in whom is my hope. He will take you out of the bird-net, and keep you safe from wasting disease. You will be covered by his feathers; under his wings you will be safe: his good faith will be your salvation.   PSALM 91:1–4 BBE

Whoever obeys his command will come to no harm, and the wise heart will know the proper time and procedure. ECCLESIASTES 8:5 NIV

He grants a treasure of good sense to the godly. He is their shield, protecting those who walk with integrity. He guards the paths of justice and protects those who are faithful to him. PROVERBS 2:7–8 NLT

"I *(Jesus)* am not asking you to take them out of the world, but I ask you to protect them from the evil one." JOHN 17:15 NRSV

Because you have made the Lord your refuge, the Most High your dwelling place, no evil shall befall you, no scourge come near your tent. For he will command his angels concerning you to guard you in all your ways. On their hands they will bear you up, so that you will not dash your foot against a stone. You will tread on the lion and the adder, the young lion and the serpent you will trample under foot. Those who love me, I will deliver; I will protect those who know my name. When they call to me, I will answer them; I will be with them in trouble, I will rescue them and honor them. With long life I will satisfy them, and show them my salvation.

PSALM 91:9–16 NRSV

Therefore take up the whole armor of God, so that you may be able to withstand on that evil day, and having done everything, to stand firm. Stand therefore, and fasten the belt of truth around your waist, and put on the breastplate of righteousness. As shoes for your feet put on whatever will make you ready to proclaim the gospel of peace. With all of these, take the shield of faith, with which you will be able to quench all the flaming arrows of the evil one. Take the helmet of salvation, and the sword of the Spirit, which is the word of God. Pray in the Spirit at all times in every prayer and supplication. To that end keep alert and always persevere in supplication for all the saints.

EPHESIANS 6:13–18 NRSV

Provider

So Abraham called the name of that place The LORD will provide; as it is said to this day, "On the mount of the LORD it shall be provided." GENESIS 22:14 RSV

"And don't worry about food—what to eat and drink. Don't worry whether God will provide it for you. These things dominate the thoughts of most people, but your Father already knows your needs. He will give you all you need from day to day if you make the Kingdom of God your primary concern."

LUKE 12:29–31 NLT

"Don't worry about things—food, drink, and clothes. For you already have life and a body—and they are far more important than what to eat and wear. Look at the birds! They don't worry about what to eat—they don't need to sow or reap or store up food—for your heavenly Father feeds them. And you are far more valuable to him than they are. Will all your worries add a single moment to your life?" MATTHEW 6:25–27 TLB

Even strong young lions sometimes go hungry, but those of us who reverence the Lord will never lack any good thing. PSALM 34:10 TLB

And why take ye thought for raiment? Consider the lilies of the field, how they grow; they toil not, neither do they spin: And yet I say unto you, That even Solomon in all his glory was not arrayed like one of these. Wherefore, if God so clothe the grass of the field, which to day is, and to morrow is cast into the oven, shall he not much more clothe you, O ye of little faith? MATTHEW 6:28–30 KJV

(Jesus said,) Up to now you have made no request in my name: do so, and it will be answered, so that your hearts may be full of joy. JOHN 16:24 BBE

For the LORD God is a sun and shield; the LORD bestows favor and honor; no good thing does he withhold from those whose walk is blameless. PSALM 84:11 NIV

I said to the LORD, "You are my Lord; apart from you I have no good thing." PSALM 16:2 NIV

I was young and now I am old, yet I have never seen the righteous forsaken or their children begging bread. They are always generous and lend freely; their children will be blessed. PSALM 37:25–26 NIV

Pure

Your eyes are too pure to behold evil, and you cannot look on wrongdoing. HABAKKUK 1:13 NRSV

The LORD despises the thoughts of the wicked, but he delights in pure words. PROVERBS 15:26 NLT

God's laws are pure, eternal, just. They are more desirable than gold. They are sweeter than honey dripping from a honeycomb. PSALM 19:9–10 TLB

How great is the love the Father has lavished on us *(who believe on Jesus),* that we should be called children of God! Everyone who has this hope in him purifies himself, just as he is pure. 1 JOHN 3:1, 3 NIV

"Blessed are the pure in heart, for they shall see God." MATTHEW 5:8 RSV

Since you have purified your souls in obeying the truth through the Spirit in sincere love of the brethren, love one another fervently with a pure heart.

1 PETER 1:22 NKJV

Pure and undefiled religion before God and the Father is this: to visit orphans and widows in their trouble, and to keep oneself unspotted from the world.

JAMES 1:27 NKJV

But the wisdom that is from above is first pure, then peaceable, gentle, willing to yield, full of mercy and good fruits, without partiality and without hypocrisy.

JAMES 3:17 NKJV

Purifying

The Lord will wash the moral filth. . . . He will cleanse. . .by a spirit of judgment that burns like fire.

ISAIAH 4:4 NLT

But who can endure the day of his coming? Who can stand when he appears? For he will be like a refiner's fire or a launderer's soap. He will sit as a refiner and purifier of silver; he will purify. . .and refine them like gold and silver. Then the LORD will have men. . .in righteousness.

MALACHI 3:2–3 NIV

"His winnowing fan is in His hand, and He will thoroughly clean out His threshing floor, and gather the wheat *(followers of Christ)* into His barn; but the chaff *(ungodly, unbelievers, sinners)* He will burn with unquenchable fire." LUKE 3:17 NKJV

To make her *(the church—those who love Jesus)* holy, cleansing her by the washing with water through the word, and to present her to himself as a radiant church, without stain or wrinkle or any other blemish, but holy and blameless. EPHESIANS 5:26–27 NIV

Purposeful

"Love the Lord your God with all your heart, and with all your soul, and with all your mind. This is the great and first commandment. And a second is like it, You shall love your neighbor as yourself."

MATTHEW 22:37–39 RSV

Someone once asked me, "Should I love God even more than my own mother?" My answer was, "Yes!"—because when a person loves God that much, their love becomes more pure and strong and selfless. A person's love for other people has much greater depth and strength and purity when they know and love God.

It is God's purpose that our way of life may be not unclean but holy.   1 THESSALONIANS 4:7 BBE

The face of the Lord is against those who do evil, To cut off the remembrance of them from the earth.

PSALM 34:16 NKJV

Is it not to give your bread to those in need, and to let the poor who have no resting-place come into your house? to put a robe on the unclothed one when you see him, and not to keep your eyes shut for fear of seeing his flesh? Then will light be shining on you like the morning, and your wounds will quickly be well: and your righteousness will go before you, and the glory of the Lord will come after you. Then at the sound of your voice, the Lord will give an answer; at your cry he will say, Here am I. If you take away from among you the yoke, the putting out of the finger of shame, and the evil word; And if you give your bread to those in need of it, so that the troubled one may have his desire; then you will have light in the dark, and your night will be as the full light of the sun: And the Lord will be your guide at all times; in dry places he will give you water in full measure, and will make strong your bones; and you will be like a watered garden, and like an ever-flowing spring.

ISAIAH 58:7–11 BBE

"I *(the Lord)* will. . .punish those who are complacent, . . .who think, 'The LORD will do nothing, either good or bad.' Their blood will be poured out like dust and their entrails like filth. Neither their silver nor their gold will be able to save them on the day of the LORD's wrath." ZEPHANIAH 1:12, 17–18 NIV

For this is the will of God, your sanctification: that you should abstain from sexual immorality.

1 THESSALONIANS 4:3 NKJV

You cry out, "Why has the LORD abandoned us?" I'll tell you why! Because the LORD witnessed the vows you and your wife made to each other on your wedding day when you were young. But you have been disloyal to her, though she remained your faithful companion, the wife of your marriage vows. Didn't the LORD make you one with your wife? In body and spirit you are his. And what does he want? Godly children from your union. So guard yourself; remain loyal to the wife of your youth. "For I hate divorce!" says the LORD, the God of Israel. "It is as cruel as putting on a victim's blood-stained coat," says the LORD Almighty. "So guard yourself; always remain loyal to your wife."

MALACHI 2:14–16 NLT

You need to persevere so that when you have done the will of God, you will receive what he has promised.

HEBREWS 10:36 NIV

"Blessed are the poor in spirit *(those who depend only on God),* for theirs is the kingdom of heaven. Blessed are those who mourn, for they will be comforted. Blessed are the meek *(humble),* for they will inherit the earth. Blessed are those who hunger and thirst for righteousness, for they will be filled. Blessed are the merciful, for they will be shown mercy. Blessed are the pure in heart, for they will see God. Blessed are the peacemakers, for they will be called sons of God. Blessed are those who are persecuted because of righteousness, for theirs is the kingdom of heaven. Blessed are you when people insult you, persecute you and falsely say all kinds of evil against you because of me *(Jesus).* Rejoice and be glad, because great is your reward in heaven."

MATTHEW 5:3–12 NIV

The world and its desires pass away, but the man who does the will of God lives forever.   1 JOHN 2:17 NIV

Quiet

But the wisdom that comes from heaven is first of all pure and full of quiet gentleness.   JAMES 3:17 TLB

Let your adornment be the inner self with the lasting beauty of a gentle and quiet spirit, which is very precious in God's sight.   1 PETER 3:4 NRSV

153

And the effect of righteousness will be peace, and the result of righteousness, quietness and trust for ever.

ISAIAH 32:17 RSV

I urge that supplications, prayers, intercessions, and thanksgivings be made for all men, for kings and all who are in high positions, that we may lead a quiet and peaceable life, godly and respectful in every way. This is good, and it is acceptable in the sight of God our Savior.

1 TIMOTHY 2:1–3 RSV

For the Lord God, . . .says: Only in returning to me and waiting for me will you be saved; in quietness and confidence is your strength.

ISAIAH 30:15 TLB

Because you have kept my word in quiet strength, I will keep you from the hour of testing which is coming on all the world.

REVELATION 3:10 BBE

Radiant

His face shone like the power of the sun in unclouded brilliance.

REVELATION 1:16 TLB

They looked to Him and were radiant.

PSALM 34:5 NKJV

Moses didn't realize. . .that his face glowed from being in the presence of God.　EXODUS 34:29 TLB

The commands of the LORD are radiant, giving light to the eyes.　PSALM 19:8 NIV

"Arise, shine, for your light has come, and the glory of the LORD rises upon you. . .The LORD rises upon you and his glory appears over you. Then you will look and be radiant, your heart will throb and swell with joy."

ISAIAH 60:1–2, 5 NIV

Suddenly, the glory of the God of Israel appeared from the east. The sound of his coming was like the roar of rushing waters, and the whole landscape shone with his glory.　EZEKIEL 43:2 NLT

Reconciler

All this is from God, who through Christ reconciled us to himself and gave us the ministry of reconciliation; that is, in Christ God was reconciling the world to himself, not counting their trespasses against them, and entrusting to us the message of reconciliation.

2 CORINTHIANS 5:18–19 RSV

And have you entirely forgotten the encouraging words God spoke to you, his children? He said, "My child, don't ignore it when the Lord disciplines you, and don't be discouraged when he corrects you. For the Lord disciplines those he loves, and he punishes those he accepts as his children." HEBREWS 12:5–6 NLT

Because the Lord wants an ongoing relationship with us, He will not ignore sin which will cut off that relationship. Confrontation from the Lord is a call to repent, with the promise of mercy and forgiveness, and a restoration of the relationship with Him.

Redeemer

I've blotted out your sins; they are gone like morning mist at noon! Oh, return to me, for I have paid the price to set you free. ISAIAH 44:22 TLB

In Him we have redemption through his blood, the forgiveness of sins, in accordance with the riches of God's grace that he lavished on us with all wisdom and understanding. EPHESIANS 1:7–8 NIV

You were not redeemed with corruptible things, like silver or gold, from your aimless conduct received by tradition from your fathers, but with the precious blood of Christ. 1 PETER 1:18–19 NKJV

Or do you not know that your body is the temple of the Holy Spirit who is in you, whom you have from God, and you are not your own? For you were bought at a price; therefore glorify God in your body and in your spirit, which are God's.   1 CORINTHIANS 6:19–20 NKJV

God bought us, those who are willing to follow Jesus, at the tremendous cost of His only Son's life.

Looking for the glad hope, the revelation of the glory of our great God and Saviour Jesus Christ; Who gave himself for us, so that he might make us free from all wrongdoing, and make for himself a people clean in heart and on fire with good works.   TITUS 2:13–14 BBE

Refuge

God is our refuge and strength, a very present help in trouble. Therefore we will not fear, though the earth should change, though the mountains shake in the heart of the sea; though its waters roar and foam, though the mountains tremble with its tumult.

PSALM 46:1–3 NRSV

I sought the LORD, and he answered me, and delivered me from all my fears.   PSALM 34:4 RSV

When you cry out, let your collection of idols deliver you! The wind will carry them off, a breath will take them away. But whoever takes refuge in me shall possess the land and inherit my holy mountain.

ISAIAH 57:13 NRSV

My God, my rock, in whom I take refuge, my shield and the horn of my salvation, my stronghold and my refuge, my savior; you save me from violence.

2 SAMUEL 22:3 NRSV

The Lord also will be a refuge for the oppressed, A refuge in times of trouble. And those who know Your name will put their trust in You; For You, Lord, have not forsaken those who seek You.   PSALM 9:9–10 NKJV

He will shield you with his wings. He will shelter you with his feathers. His faithful promises are your armor and protection.   PSALM 91:4 NLT

Because thou hast made the LORD, which is my refuge, even the most High, thy habitation; There shall no evil befall thee, neither shall any plague come nigh thy dwelling. For he shall give his angels charge over thee, to keep thee in all thy ways. They shall bear thee up in their hands, lest thou dash thy foot against a stone. Thou shalt tread upon the lion and adder: the young lion and the dragon shalt thou trample under feet.

Because he hath set his love upon me, therefore will I deliver him: I will set him on high, because he hath known my name. He shall call upon me, and I will answer him: I will be with him in trouble; I will deliver him, and honour him. With long life will I satisfy him, and shew him my salvation.   PSALM 91:9–16 KJV

Reliable
See "Dependable" and "Truth."

None who have faith in God will ever be disgraced for trusting him.   PSALM 25:3 TLB

Rescuer

But now, says the Lord. . . : have no fear, for I have taken up your cause *(those who know Jesus as their Savior)*; naming you by your name, I have made you mine. When you go through the waters, I will be with you; and through the rivers, they will not go over you: when you go through the fire, you will not be burned; and the flame will have no power over you. For I am the Lord your God, the Holy One of Israel, your saviour.
     ISAIAH 43:1–3 BBE

"As I was with Moses, so I will be with you; I will not fail you or forsake you." JOSHUA 1:5 RSV

He sent from above, He took me; He drew me out of many waters. He delivered me from my strong enemy, From those who hated me, For they were too strong for me. PSALM 18:16–17 NKJV

Praise be to the LORD, for he showed his wonderful love to me when I was in a besieged city. In my alarm I said, "I am cut off from your sight!" Yet you heard my cry for mercy when I called to you for help.
PSALM 31:21–22 NIV

And after you have suffered for a little while, the God of all grace, who has called you to his eternal glory in Christ, will himself restore, support, strengthen, and establish you. 1 PETER 5:10 NRSV

God is our refuge and strength, a very present help in trouble. Therefore will not we fear, though the earth be removed, and though the mountains be carried into the midst of the sea; Though the waters thereof roar and be troubled, though the mountains shake with the swelling thereof. . . . He maketh wars to cease unto the end of the earth; he breaketh the bow, and cut-teth the spear in sunder; he burneth the chariot in the fire. Be still, and know that I am God: I will be exalted among the heathen, I will be exalted in the earth.
PSALM 46:1–3, 9–10 KJV

Strengthen the weak hands, And make firm the feeble knees. Say to those who are fearful-hearted, "Be strong, do not fear! Behold, your God will come with vengeance, With the recompense of God; He will come and save you." Then the eyes of the blind shall be opened, And the ears of the deaf shall be unstopped. Then the lame shall leap like a deer, And the tongue of the dumb sing. For waters shall burst forth in the wilderness, And streams in the desert. The parched ground shall become a pool, And the thirsty land springs of water; In the habitation of jackals, where each lay, There shall be grass with reeds and rushes. A highway shall be there, and a road, and it shall be called the Highway of Holiness. The unclean shall not pass over it, But it shall be for others. Whoever walks the road, although a fool, Shall not go astray. No lion shall be there, Nor shall any ravenous beast go up on it; It shall not be found there. But the redeemed shall walk there, And the ransomed of the Lord shall return, And come to Zion with singing, With everlasting joy on their heads. They shall obtain joy and gladness, And sorrow and sighing shall flee away.   ISAIAH 35:3–10 NKJV

Responsive

Come near to God and he will come near to you.

JAMES 4:8 BBE

If you had responded to my rebuke, I would have poured out my heart to you and made my thoughts known to you.   PROVERBS 1:23 NIV

"For the Lord your God is gracious and merciful, and will not turn His face from you if you return to Him."
                                        2 CHRONICLES 30:9 NKJV

"If you seek him, you will find him. But if you forsake him, he will reject you forever."   1 CHRONICLES 28:9 NLT

"If My people who are called by My name will humble themselves, and pray and seek My face, and turn from their wicked ways, then I will hear from heaven, and will forgive their sin and heal their land."
                                        2 CHRONICLES 7:14 NKJV

"If you then, who are evil, know how to give good gifts to your children, how much more will your Father who is in heaven give good things to those who ask him!"
                                        MATTHEW 7:11 RSV

Let your cry come to me, and I will give you an answer, and let you see great things and secret things of which you had no knowledge.   JEREMIAH 33:3 BBE

The friendship of the LORD is for those who fear him, and he makes known to them his covenant.
                                        PSALM 25:14 RSV

The earnest prayer of a righteous person has great power and wonderful results.   JAMES 5:16 NLT

The earth and everything in it and above it are the Lord's. He who has clean hands and a pure heart stands in the Lord's holy place. The prayer of a righteous man is very powerful and effective! (See Psalms 15 and 24.)

Water closed over my head; I said, "I am lost." I called on your name, O Lord, from the depths of the pit; you heard my plea, "Do not close your ear to my cry for help, but give me relief!" You came near when I called on you; you said, "Do not fear!" You have taken up my cause, O Lord, you have redeemed my life.

LAMENTATIONS 3:54–58 NRSV

Revenger

Don't repay evil for evil. Wait for the Lord to handle the matter.   PROVERBS 20:22 TLB

For we have had experience of him who says, Punishment is mine, I will give reward. And again, The Lord will be judge of his people. We may well go in fear of falling into the hands of the living God.

HEBREWS 10:30–31 BBE

The Lord is living; praise be to my Rock, and let the God of my salvation be honoured: It is God who sends punishment on my haters, and puts peoples under my rule. He makes me free from my haters: I am lifted up over those who come up against me: you have made me free from the violent man.   2 SAMUEL 22:47–49 BBE

Do not take away the property of the poor man because he is poor, or be cruel to the crushed ones when they come before the judge: For the Lord will give support to their cause, and take the life of those who take their goods.   PROVERBS 22:22–23 BBE

Whoever shuts his ears to the cry of the poor Will also cry himself and not be heard.   PROVERBS 21:13 NKJV

Do not give punishment for wrongs done to you, dear brothers, but give way to the wrath of God; for it is said in the holy Writings, Punishment is mine, I will give reward, says the Lord. But if one who has hate for you is in need of food or of drink, give it to him, for in so doing you will put coals of fire on his head. Do not let evil overcome you, but overcome evil by good.

ROMANS 12:19–21 BBE

Do not rejoice when your enemy falls, And do not let your heart be glad when he stumbles; lest the Lord see it, and it displease Him, And He turn away His wrath from him.   PROVERBS 24:17–18 NKJV

O LORD God, to whom vengeance belongeth; O God, to whom vengeance belongeth, shew thyself. Lift up thyself, thou judge of the earth: render a reward to the proud. LORD, how long shall the wicked, how long shall the wicked triumph? PSALM 94:1–3 KJV

Reward

"I *(the Lord)* am your shield, your exceedingly great reward." GENESIS 15:1 NKJV

The sting of death is sin, and the power of sin is the law. But thanks be to God, who gives us the victory through our Lord Jesus Christ. Therefore, my beloved, be steadfast, immovable, always excelling in the work of the Lord, because you know that in the Lord your labor is not in vain. 1 CORINTHIANS 15:56–58 NRSV

Rewarder

Take delight in the LORD, and he will give you the desires of your heart. PSALM 37:4 RSV

The Lord God is our sun and our strength: the Lord will give grace and glory: he will not keep back any good thing from those whose ways are upright.

PSALM 84:11 BBE

He will fulfill the desire of those who fear Him; He also will hear their cry and save them. The Lord preserves all who love Him, But all the wicked He will destroy.   PSALM 145:19–20 NKJV

But let your first care be for his kingdom and his righteousness; and all these other things will be given to you in addition.   MATTHEW 6:33 BBE

But without faith it is impossible to please Him, for he who comes to God must believe that He is, and that He is a rewarder of those who diligently seek Him.
                    HEBREWS 11:6 NKJV

"But when you do a kindness to someone, do it secretly —don't tell your left hand what your right hand is doing. And your Father who knows all secrets will reward you."   MATTHEW 6:3–4 TLB

"But love your enemies, do good, and lend, expecting nothing in return. Your reward will be great, and you will be children of the Most High; for he is kind to the ungrateful and the wicked."

                    LUKE 6:35 NRSV

"And all these blessings shall come upon you and overtake you, because you obey the voice of the Lord your God."   DEUTERONOMY 28:2 NKJV

Give, and it will be given to you; good measure, crushed down, full and running over, they will give to you. For in the same measure as you give, it will be given to you again.   LUKE 6:38 BBE

"Assuredly, I say to you, there is no one who has left house or parents or brothers or wife or children, for the sake of the kingdom of God, who shall not receive many times more in this present time, and in the age to come eternal life."   LUKE 18:29–30 NKJV

For if we keep the substance of the faith which we had at the start, even till the end, we have a part with Christ.   HEBREWS 3:14 BBE

Therefore do not cast away your confidence, which has great reward. For you have need of endurance, so that after you have done the will of God, you may receive the promise.   HEBREWS 10:35–36 NKJV

"Because you have kept my word of patient endurance, I will keep you from the hour of trial that is coming on the whole world to test the inhabitants of the earth."   REVELATION 3:10 NRSV

Righteous

For the Lord is righteous, He loves righteousness; His countenance beholds the upright.   PSALM 11:7 NKJV

The LORD is righteous in all his ways and loving toward all he has made.   PSALM 145:17 NIV

Righteousness and justice are the foundation of Your throne; Mercy and truth go before Your face.

PSALM 89:14 NKJV

Unfailing love and faithfulness cover sin; evil is avoided by fear of the LORD.   PROVERBS 16:6 NLT

The sacrifice of the wicked is an abomination to the Lord, but the prayer of the upright is his delight. The way of the wicked is an abomination to the Lord, but he loves the one who pursues righteousness.

PROVERBS 15:8–9 NRSV

For the eyes of the Lord are intently watching all who live good lives, and he gives attention when they cry to him. But the Lord has made up his mind to wipe out even the memory of evil men from the earth. Yes, the Lord hears the good man when he calls to him for help, and saves him out of all his troubles.

PSALM 34:15–17 TLB

"Your throne, O God, is forever and ever; A scepter of righteousness is the scepter of Your kingdom. You have loved righteousness and hated lawlessness."

HEBREWS 1:8–9 NKJV

For see, the day is coming, it is burning like an oven; all the men of pride and all who do evil will be dry stems of grass: and in the day which is coming they will be burned up, says the Lord of armies, till they have not a root or a branch. But to you who give worship to my name, the sun of righteousness will come up with new life in its wings; and you will go out, playing like young oxen full of food.

MALACHI 4:1–2 BBE

Great and full of wonder are your works, O Lord God, Ruler of all; true and full of righteousness are your ways, eternal King. What man is there who will not have fear before you, O Lord, and give glory to your name? because you only are holy; for all the nations will come and give worship before you; for your righteousness has been made clear.

REVELATION 15:3–4 BBE

You answer us with awesome deeds of righteousness, O God our Savior, the hope of all the ends of the earth and of the farthest seas.

PSALM 65:5 NIV

Rock

Lord, how I love you! For you have done such tremendous things for me. The Lord is my fort where I can enter and be safe; no one can follow me in and slay me. He is a rugged mountain where I hide; he is my Savior, a rock where none can reach me, and a tower of safety. He is my shield.   PSALM 18:1–2 TLB

A voice said, "Shout!" I asked, "What should I shout?" "Shout that people are like the grass that dies away. Their beauty fades as quickly as the beauty of flowers in a field. The grass withers, and the flowers fade beneath the breath of the LORD. And so it is with people. The grass withers, and the flowers fade, but the word of our God stands forever."   ISAIAH 40:6–8 NLT

Now to him who is able to keep you from falling, and to give you a place in his glory, free from all evil, with great joy, To the only God our Saviour, through Jesus Christ our Lord, let us give glory and honour and authority and power, before all time and now and for ever. So be it.   JUDE 24–25 BBE

The Lord is upright; he is my Rock, there is no deceit in him.   PSALM 92:15 BBE

"The LORD is my rock, and my fortress, and my deliverer."   2 SAMUEL 22:2 RSV

" 'You are my Father, my God, and the Rock of my salvation!' " PSALM 89:26 NRSV

Safety

I will both lie down in peace, and sleep; For You alone, O Lord, make me dwell in safety.

PSALM 4:8 NKJV

The fear of man is a cause of danger: but whoever puts his faith in the Lord will have a safe place on high.

PROVERBS 29:25 BBE

"But whoever listens to me will dwell safely, And will be secure, without fear of evil."

PROVERBS 1:33 NKJV

Sanctifier

May the God of peace himself sanctify you entirely; and may your spirit and soul and body be kept sound and blameless at the coming of our Lord Jesus Christ. The one who calls you is faithful, and he will do this.

1 THESSALONIANS 5:23–24 NRSV

"Sanctify them in the truth; your word is truth."

JOHN 17:17 NRSV

As we study and meditate on God's Word to us, the Holy Bible, we become sanctified when we obey.

Satisfier

All the riches, all the fun and pleasure, all the knowledge, all the fame and status, all the relationships—none can totally satisfy a person.

I gathered me also silver and gold, and the peculiar treasure of kings and of the provinces: I gat me men singers and women singers, and the delights of the sons of men, as musical instruments, and that of all sorts. So I was great, and increased more than all that were before me in Jerusalem: also my wisdom remained with me. And whatsoever mine eyes desired I kept not from them, I withheld not my heart from any joy; for my heart rejoiced in all my labour: and this was my portion of all my labour. Then I looked on all the works that my hands had wrought, and on the labour that I had laboured to do: and, behold, all was vanity and vexation of spirit, and there was no profit under the sun.

ECCLESIASTES 2:8–11 KJV

A single day spent in your Temple is better than a thousand anywhere else! I would rather be a doorman of the Temple of my God than live in palaces of wickedness. For Jehovah God is our Light and our Protector. He gives us grace and glory. No good thing will he withhold from those who walk along his paths.

PSALM 84:10–11 TLB

Savior

O LORD, the God who saves me. . .   PSALM 88:1 NIV

Who told this long ago? Who declared it of old? Was it not I, the Lord? There is no other god besides me, a righteous God and a Savior; there is no one besides me. Turn to me and be saved, all the ends of the earth! For I am God, and there is no other.   ISAIAH 45:21–22 NRSV

The Father sent his Son to be the Savior of the world. All who proclaim that Jesus is the Son of God have God living in them, and they live in God. We know how much God loves us, and we have put our trust in him. God is love, and all who live in love live in God, and God lives in them.   1 JOHN 4:14–16 NLT

And now, all glory to God, who is able to keep you from stumbling, and who will bring you into his glorious presence innocent of sin and with great joy. All glory to him, who alone is God our Savior, through Jesus Christ our Lord. Yes, glory, majesty, power, and authority belong to him, in the beginning, now, and forevermore.

JUDE 24–25 NLT

And it shall come to pass in the last days, saith God, . . .I will shew wonders in heaven above, and signs in the earth beneath; blood, and fire, and vapour of smoke: The sun shall be turned into darkness, and the moon into blood, before that great and notable day of the Lord come: And it shall come to pass, that whosoever shall call on the name of the Lord shall be saved.

ACTS 2:17, 19–21 KJV

Do not give me up, O Lord; O my God, be near to me. Come quickly to give me help, O Lord, my salvation.

PSALM 38:21–22 BBE

Searching

"I will search with lanterns in. . .darkest corners to find and punish those who sit contented in their sins, indifferent to God, thinking he will let them alone."

ZEPHANIAH 1:12 TLB

The LORD'S searchlight penetrates the human spirit, exposing every hidden motive.   PROVERBS 20:27 NLT

For the eyes of the Lord are intently watching all who live good lives, and he gives attention when they cry to him. But the Lord has made up his mind to wipe out even the memory of evil men from the earth. Yes, the Lord hears the good man when he calls to him for help, and saves him out of all his troubles.

PSALM 34:15–17 TLB

But we know these things because God has revealed them to us by his Spirit, and his Spirit searches out everything and shows us even God's deep secrets.

1 CORINTHIANS 2:10 NLT

Self-existent

All created things originated somewhere at sometime— but God has no origin.

God replied, "I AM THE ONE WHO ALWAYS IS. Just tell them, 'I AM has sent me to you.' "

EXODUS 3:14 NLT

Shepherd

Because the Lord is my Shepherd, I have everything I need! He lets me rest in the meadow grass and leads me beside the quiet streams. He restores my failing health. He helps me do what honors him the most. Even when walking through the dark valley of death I will not be afraid, for you are close beside me, guarding, guiding all the way.   PSALM 23:1–4 TLB

When the Chief Shepherd appears, you will receive the crown of glory that does not fade away.

1 PETER 5:4 NKJV

For this is what the Lord has said: Truly, I, even I, will go searching and looking for my sheep. As the keeper goes looking for his flock when he is among his wandering sheep, so I will go looking for my sheep, and will get them safely out of all the places where they have been sent wandering in the day of clouds and black night.   EZEKIEL 34:11–12 BBE

Shield
See "Protector."

Yes, our protection is from the Lord himself.

PSALM 89:18 TLB

The Lord is my strength and my shield; My heart trusted in Him, and I am helped; Therefore my heart greatly rejoices, And with my song I will praise Him.

PSALM 28:7 NKJV

In the shelter of your presence you hide them from human plots; you hold them safe under your shelter from contentious tongues.

PSALM 31:20 NRSV

But You, O Lord, are a shield for me, My glory and the One who lifts up my head. I cried to the Lord with my voice, And He heard me from His holy hill.

PSALM 3:3–4 NKJV

For the Lord God is a sun and shield; the Lord will give grace and glory; No good thing will He withhold From those who walk uprightly.

PSALM 84:11 NKJV

Sincere

But the wisdom that comes from heaven is first of all pure. It is also peace loving, gentle at all times, and willing to yield to others. It is full of mercy and good deeds. It shows no partiality and is always sincere.

JAMES 3:17 NLT

Greater love has no man than this, that a man gives up his life for his friends.   JOHN 15:13 BBE

Song

For you have been my help, and in the shadow of your wings I sing for joy.   PSALM 63:7 NRSV

The Lord is my strength, my song, and my salvation.   EXODUS 15:2 TLB

I will sing of your steadfast love, O Lord, forever.   PSALM 89:1 NRSV

"I will sing to the LORD, for he has triumphed gloriously."   EXODUS 15:1 RSV

Shout for joy to the LORD, all the earth, burst into jubilant song with music.   PSALM 98:4 NIV

Let the sea roar, and all that fills it; the world and those who live in it. Let the floods clap their hands; let the hills sing together for joy at the presence of the Lord, for he is coming to judge the earth. He will judge the world with righteousness, and the peoples with equity.   PSALM 98:7–9 NRSV

But You are holy, Enthroned in the praises of Israel.

PSALM 22:3 NKJV

Israel here is the spiritual family of all who know Jesus as Lord and Savior, not the physical nation of Israel.

Not all who are descended from Israel are Israel. Nor because they are his descendants are they all Abraham's children. . . . In other words, it is not the natural children who are God's children, but it is the children of the promise *(people who believe God's promise of eternal life through Jesus Christ)* who are regarded as Abraham's offspring.

ROMANS 9:6–8 NIV

Sing unto God, ye kingdoms of the earth; O sing praises unto the Lord; Selah: To him that rideth upon the heavens of heavens, which were of old; lo, he doth send out his voice, and that a mighty voice. Ascribe ye strength unto God: his excellency is over Israel, and his strength is in the clouds. O God, thou art terrible out of thy holy places: the God of Israel is he that giveth strength and power unto his people.

PSALM 68:32–35 KJV

"The Lord your God in your midst, The Mighty One, will save; He will rejoice over you with gladness, He will quiet you with His love, He will rejoice over you with singing."

ZEPHANIAH 3:17 NKJV

179

Praise the Lord! Praise God in his sanctuary; praise him in his mighty firmament! Praise him for his mighty deeds; praise him according to his surpassing greatness! Praise him with trumpet sound; praise him with lute and harp! Praise him with tambourine and dance; praise him with strings and pipe! Praise him with clanging cymbals; praise him with loud clashing cymbals! Let everything that breathes praise the Lord! Praise the Lord!

PSALM 150:1–6 NRSV

Sovereign

"Sovereign Lord, holy and true, . . ."

REVELATION 6:10 RSV

"God Most High, Creator of heaven and earth. . ."

GENESIS 14:19 NLT

"Lord, the God of heaven and the God of the earth. . ."

GENESIS 24:3 NKJV

God of gods! . . . Lord of lords! . . . To Him who alone does great wonders.

PSALM 136:2–4 NKJV

"Lord of hosts, . . .You are God, You alone, of all the kingdoms of the earth. You have made heaven and earth."

ISAIAH 37:16 NKJV

"I am the First and Last; there is no other God."

ISAIAH 44:6 TLB

Who told this long ago? Who declared it of old? Was it not I, the Lord? There is no other god besides me, a righteous God and a Savior; there is no one besides me. Turn to me and be saved, all the ends of the earth! For I am God, and there is no other.   ISAIAH 45:21–22 NRSV

"How great you are, O Sovereign LORD! There is no one like you—there is no other God. We have never even heard of another god like you!"

2 SAMUEL 7:22 NLT

And now—all glory to him who alone is God, who saves us through Jesus Christ our Lord; yes, splendor and majesty, all power and authority are his from the beginning; his they are and his they evermore shall be.

JUDE 1:24–25 TLB

Spirit

"God is Spirit, and those who worship Him must worship in spirit and truth."   JOHN 4:24 NKJV

"The Kingdom of God isn't ushered in with visible signs. You won't be able to say, 'It has begun here in this place or there in that part of the country.' For the Kingdom of God is within you."   LUKE 17:20–21 TLB

Now the Lord is the Spirit: and where the Spirit of the Lord is, there the heart is free.   2 CORINTHIANS 3:17 BBE

"The true worshipers will worship the Father in spirit and truth, for the Father seeks such as these to worship him."   JOHN 4:23 NRSV

The fruit of the Spirit is love, joy, peace, patience, kindness, generosity, faithfulness, gentleness, and self-control.   GALATIANS 5:22–23 NRSV

Search me, O God, and know my heart; test my thoughts. Point out anything you find in me that makes you sad, and lead me along the path of everlasting life.
PSALM 139:23–24 TLB

Splendid

Honor and majesty surround him; strength and beauty are in his sanctuary.   PSALM 96:6 NLT

Give honor to the LORD for the glory of his name. Worship the LORD in the splendor of his holiness.
PSALM 29:2 NLT

Let them praise the name of the Lord, For His name alone is exalted; His glory is above the earth and heaven.   PSALM 148:13 NKJV

Let each generation tell its children of your mighty acts. I will meditate on your majestic, glorious splendor and your wonderful miracles. Your awe-inspiring deeds will be on every tongue; I will proclaim your greatness. Everyone will share the story of your wonderful goodness; they will sing with joy of your righteousness.

PSALM 145:4–7 NLT

"For as we cannot look at the sun for its brightness when the winds have cleared away the clouds, neither can we gaze at the terrible majesty of God breaking forth upon us from heaven, clothed in dazzling splendor. We cannot imagine the power of the Almighty, and yet he is so just and merciful that he does not destroy us." JOB 37:21–23 TLB

Steadfast

Let us not become weary in doing good, for at the proper time we will reap a harvest if we do not give up.

GALATIANS 6:9 NIV

For I am convinced that neither death, nor life, nor angels, nor rulers, nor things present, nor things to come, nor powers, nor height, nor depth, nor anything else in all creation, will be able to separate us from the love of God in Christ Jesus our Lord.

ROMANS 8:38–39 NRSV

Now it is God who makes both us and you stand firm in Christ. 2 CORINTHIANS 1:21 NIV

Strategist

God causes everything to work together for the good of those who love God. ROMANS 8:28 NLT

The human mind may devise many plans, but it is the purpose of the Lord that will be established.

PROVERBS 19:21 NRSV

The LORD works out everything for his own ends— even the wicked for a day of disaster.

PROVERBS 16:4 NIV

Give no thought to the things which are past; let the early times go out of your minds. See, I am doing a new thing; now it is starting; will you not take note of it? I will even make a way in the waste land, and rivers in the dry country. ISAIAH 43:18–19 BBE

For surely I know the plans I have for you, says the Lord, plans for your welfare and not for harm, to give you a future with hope. Then when you call upon me and come and pray to me, I will hear you. When you search for me, you will find me; if you seek me with all your heart. JEREMIAH 29:11–13 NRSV

"You meant evil against me; but God meant it for good."   GENESIS 50:20 NKJV

Make yourselves holy, for tomorrow the Lord will do works of wonder among you.   JOSHUA 3:5 BBE

You have multiplied, O Lord my God, your wondrous deeds and your thoughts toward us; none can compare with you. Were I to proclaim and tell of them, they would be more than can be counted.   PSALM 40:5 NRSV

Strength

Honor and majesty are before Him; Strength and beauty are in His sanctuary.   PSALM 96:6 NKJV

O my strength, I will watch for you; for you, O God, are my fortress.   PSALM 59:9 NRSV

The Lord is my light and my salvation; whom shall I fear? The Lord is the stronghold of my life; of whom shall I be afraid?   PSALM 27:1 NRSV

You are their glorious strength. Our power is based on your favor.   PSALM 89:17 NLT

"The joy of the Lord is your strength."

NEHEMIAH 8:10 NKJV

The Lord God is my Strength, and he will give me the speed of a deer and bring me safely over the mountains.

HABAKKUK 3:19 TLB

Blessed are those who have learned to acclaim you, who walk in the light of your presence, O LORD. They rejoice in Your name all day long; they exult in Your righteousness. For you are their glory and strength, and by your favor you exalt our horn.   PSALM 89:15–17 NIV

Have you no knowledge of it? has it not come to your ears? The eternal God, the Lord, the Maker of the ends of the earth, is never feeble or tired; there is no searching out of his wisdom. He gives power to the feeble, increasing the strength of him who has no force. Even the young men will become feeble and tired, and the best of them will come to the end of his strength; But those who are waiting for the Lord will have new strength; they will get wings like eagles: running, they will not be tired, and walking, they will have no weariness.   ISAIAH 40:28–31 BBE

Sudden

And in an instant, suddenly, you will be visited by the Lord of hosts with thunder and earthquake and great noise, with whirlwind and tempest, and the flame of a devouring fire.   ISAIAH 29:5–6 NRSV

Behold, these are the ungodly, who prosper in the world; they increase in riches. When I thought to know this, it was too painful for me; Until I went into the sanctuary of God; then understood I their end. How are they brought into desolation, as in a moment! they are utterly consumed with terrors.

PSALM 73:12, 16–17, 19 KJV

They search out iniquities; they accomplish a diligent search: both the inward thought of every one of them, and the heart, is deep. But God shall shoot at them with an arrow; suddenly shall they be wounded. So they shall make their own tongue to fall upon them-selves: all that see them shall flee away.

PSALM 64:6–8 KJV

"Time and again I *(the Lord)* warned you about what was going to happen in the future. Then suddenly I took action, and all my predictions came true."

ISAIAH 48:3 NLT

"The Lord, whom you seek, Will suddenly come to His temple, Even the Messenger of the covenant, In whom you delight. Behold, He is coming."   MALACHI 3:1 NKJV

For you yourselves know very well that the day of the Lord will come like a thief in the night. When they say, "There is peace and security," then sudden destruction will come upon them.   1 THESSALONIANS 5:2–3 NRSV

And suddenly from heaven there came a sound like the rush of a violent wind, and it filled the entire house where they were sitting. Divided tongues, as of fire, appeared among them, and a tongue rested on each of them. All of them were filled with the Holy Spirit and began to speak in other languages, as the Spirit gave them ability.   ACTS 2:2–4 NRSV

So you are to keep watch: because you are not certain when the master of the house *(Jesus)* is coming, in the evening, or in the middle of the night, or at the cock's cry, or in the morning; For fear that, coming suddenly, he sees you sleeping.   MARK 13:35–36 BBE

Sufficient

And He said to me, "My grace is sufficient for you, for My strength is made perfect in weakness."

2 CORINTHIANS 12:9 NKJV

It is not that we think we can do anything of lasting value by ourselves. Our only power and success come from God.   2 CORINTHIANS 3:5 NLT

And my God shall supply all your need according to His riches in glory by Christ Jesus.

PHILIPPIANS 4:19 NKJV

All Scripture is inspired by God and is useful to teach us what is true and to make us realize what is wrong in our lives. It straightens us out and teaches us to do what is right. It is God's way of preparing us in every way, fully equipped for every good thing God wants us to do. 2 TIMOTHY 3:16–17 NLT

As we know Jesus better, his divine power gives us every-thing we need for living a godly life. He has called us to receive his own glory and goodness! 2 PETER 1:3 NLT

I know how to live on almost nothing or with every-thing. I have learned the secret of contentment in every situation, whether it be a full stomach or hunger, plenty or want; for I can do everything God asks me to with the help of Christ who gives me the strength and power. PHILIPPIANS 4:12–13 TLB

" 'Not by might nor by power, but by My Spirit,' says the Lord of hosts." ZECHARIAH 4:6 NKJV

Supernatural

"He has come from above and is greater than anyone else. I am of the earth, and my understanding is limited to the things of earth, but he has come from heaven."

JOHN 3:31 NLT

And He *(Jesus)* said to them, "You are from beneath; I am from above. You are of this world; I am not of this world." JOHN 8:23 NKJV

And it shall come to pass in the last days, saith God, I will pour out of my Spirit upon all flesh: and your sons and your daughters shall prophesy, and your young men shall see visions, and your old men shall dream dreams: And on my servants and on my handmaidens I will pour out in those days of my Spirit; and they shall prophesy: And I will shew wonders in heaven above, and signs in the earth beneath; blood, and fire, and vapour of smoke: The sun shall be turned into darkness, and the moon into blood. ACTS 2:17–20 KJV

Support
See "Helper," "Refuge," "Rock," "Strength."

It is God who gives us, along with you, the ability to stand firm for Christ. He has commissioned us, and he has identified us as his own by placing the Holy Spirit in our hearts as the first installment of everything he will give us. 2 CORINTHIANS 1:21–22 NLT

Supreme
See "Incomparable," "Sovereign," "Transcendent."

Sympathetic

Come to me, all you who are troubled and weighted down with care, and I will give you rest.

MATTHEW 11:28 BBE

He upholds the cause of the oppressed and gives food to the hungry. The LORD sets prisoners free, the LORD gives sight to the blind, the LORD lifts up those who are bowed down, the LORD loves the righteous. The LORD watches over the alien and sustains the fatherless and the widow, but he frustrates the ways of the wicked.

PSALM 146:7–9 NIV

For we do not have a high priest *(Jesus)* who is unable to sympathize with our weaknesses, but we have one who in every respect has been tested as we are, yet without sin.

HEBREWS 4:15 NRSV

Teacher

"Behold, God is exalted by His power; Who teaches like Him?"

JOB 36:22 NKJV

I will instruct you *(those who seek the Lord)* and teach you the way you should go; I will counsel you with my eye upon you.   PSALM 32:8 NRSV

Come, my children, listen to me; I will teach you the fear of the LORD. Whoever of you loves life and desires to see many good days, keep your tongue from evil and your lips from speaking lies. Turn from evil and do good; seek peace and pursue it.   PSALM 34:11–14 NIV

Thus says the Lord, your Redeemer, the Holy One of Israel: I am the Lord your God, who teaches you for your own good, who leads you in the way you should go. O that you had paid attention to my command-ments! Then your prosperity would have been like a river, and your success like the waves of the sea.

ISAIAH 48:17–18 NRSV

The whole Bible was given to us by inspiration from God and is useful to teach us what is true and to make us realize what is wrong in our lives; it straightens us out and helps us do what is right.

2 TIMOTHY 3:16–17 TLB

[God] also made us sufficient as ministers of the new covenant, not of the letter but of the Spirit; for the let-ter kills, but the Spirit gives life.

2 CORINTHIANS 3:6 NKJV

Tester

We are not trying to please men but God, who tests our hearts.　　　　1 THESSALONIANS 2:4 NIV

Search me, O God, and know my heart; test me and know my anxious thoughts. See if there is any offensive way in me, and lead me in the way everlasting.
　　　　PSALM 139:23–24 NIV

"But He knows the way that I take; When He has tested me, I shall come forth as gold. My foot has held fast to His steps; I have kept His way and not turned aside. I have not departed from the commandment of His lips; I have treasured the words of His mouth More than my necessary food."　　　　JOB 23:10–12 NKJV

Transcendent

The High and Lofty One Who inhabits eternity. . .
　　　　ISAIAH 57:15 NKJV

"For My thoughts are not your thoughts, Nor are your ways My ways," says the Lord. "For as the heavens are higher than the earth, So are My ways higher than your ways, And My thoughts than your thoughts."
　　　　ISAIAH 55:8–9 NKJV

Trinity

God is three persons in one: God the Father, God the Son (Jesus Christ), and God the Holy Spirit.

"Baptizing them in the name of the Father and of the Son and of the Holy Spirit. . ."   MATTHEW 28:19 RSV

The three are seen operating together in Hebrews 9:14, where Christ, through the Holy Spirit, offered Himself without sin to God.

How much more, . . .will the blood of Christ, who through the eternal Spirit offered himself unblemished to God, cleanse our consciences from acts that lead to death, so that we may serve the living God!

HEBREWS 9:14 NIV

The salvation of any person is the work of all three:

Who have been chosen and destined by God the Father and sanctified by the Spirit to be obedient to Jesus Christ and to be sprinkled with his blood.

1 PETER 1:2 NRSV

"I *(Jesus)* and My Father are one."   JOHN 10:30 NKJV

"The Lord our God, the Lord is one!"

DEUTERONOMY 6:4 NKJV

The indwelling of the Christian is by all three—the Father, the Son, and the Holy Spirit:

"I *(Jesus)* will ask the Father and he will give you another Comforter, and he will never leave you. He is the Holy Spirit, the Spirit who leads into all truth. . . . I will only reveal myself to those who love me and obey me. The Father will love them too, and we will come to them and live with them."   JOHN 14:15–17, 23 TLB

True

But the Lord is the true God; He is the living God and the everlasting King. At His wrath the earth will tremble, And the nations will not be able to endure His indignation.   JEREMIAH 10:10 NKJV

"And this is eternal life, that they may know You, the only true God, and Jesus Christ whom You have sent."   JOHN 17:3 NKJV

And we are certain that the Son of God has come, and has given us a clear vision, so that we may see him who is true, and we are in him who is true, in his Son Jesus Christ. He is the true God and eternal life.

1 JOHN 5:20 BBE

They keep telling us about the wonderful welcome you gave us, and how you turned away from your idols to God so that now the living and true God only is your Master. And they speak of how you are looking forward to the return of God's Son from heaven—Jesus, whom God brought back to life—and he is our only Savior from God's terrible anger against sin.

1 THESSALONIANS 1:9–10 TLB

You are near, O LORD, And all Your commandments are truth. PSALM 119:151 NKJV

All your words are true; all your righteous laws are eternal. PSALM 119:160 NIV

They called loudly to the Lord and said, "O Sovereign Lord, holy and true, how long will it be before you judge the people of the earth for what they've done to us?" REVELATION 6:10 TLB

"Thus says the Lord of hosts: 'Execute true justice, Show mercy and compassion.' " ZECHARIAH 7:9 NKJV

My mouth speaks what is true, for my lips detest wickedness. PROVERBS 8:7 NIV

"Great and marvelous are Your works, Lord God Almighty! Just and true are Your ways, O King of the saints!" REVELATION 15:3 NKJV

"Yes, O Lord God, the Almighty, your judgments are true and just!"   REVELATION 16:7 NRSV

Trustworthy

Put not your trust in princes, nor in the son of man, in whom there is no help. His breath goeth forth, he returneth to his earth; in that very day his thoughts perish. Happy is he that hath the God of Jacob for his help, whose hope is in the LORD his God: Which made heaven, and earth, the sea, and all that therein is: which keepeth truth for ever.   PSALM 146:3–6 KJV

The fear of man brings a snare, But whoever trusts in the Lord shall be safe.   PROVERBS 29:25 NKJV

Your word, O LORD, is eternal; it stands firm in the heavens.   PSALM 119:89 NIV

In you our fathers put their trust; they trusted and you delivered them. They cried to you and were saved; in you they trusted and were not disappointed.

PSALM 22:4–5 NIV

Who among you fears the LORD and obeys his servant? If you are walking in darkness, without a ray of light, trust in the LORD and rely on your God.

ISAIAH 50:10 NLT

For God cannot be tempted by evil, nor does he tempt anyone.   JAMES 1:13 NIV

I saw heaven standing open and there before me was a white horse, whose rider is called Faithful and True. With justice he judges and makes war.

REVELATION 19:11 NIV

Truth

These are the things that you shall do: Speak the truth to one another, render in your gates judgments that are true and make for peace, do not devise evil in your hearts against one another, and love no false oath; for all these are things that I hate, says the Lord.

ZECHARIAH 8:16–17 NRSV

God, who cannot lie, . . .   TITUS 1:2 NKJV

O LORD, the God of truth. . .   PSALM 31:5 NIV

You desire truth in the inward being; therefore teach me wisdom in my secret heart.   PSALM 51:6 NRSV

The LORD detests lying lips, but he delights in men who are truthful.   PROVERBS 12:22 NIV

Whoever invokes a blessing in the land will do so by the God of truth; he who takes an oath in the land will swear by the God of truth.   ISAIAH 65:16 NIV

"Sanctify them in the truth; your word is truth."
                                                                    JOHN 17:17 NRSV

For the word of the Lord is right, And all His work is done in truth. He loves righteousness and justice.
                                                            PSALM 33:4–5 NKJV

"God is not a human being, that he should lie, or a mortal, that he should change his mind. Has he promised, and will he not do it? Has he spoken, and will he not fulfill it? See, I received a command to bless; he has blessed, and I cannot revoke it."
                                                        NUMBERS 23:19–20 NRSV

Unapproachable

He who is the blessed and only Sovereign, the King of kings and Lord of lords. It is he alone who has immortality and dwells in unapproachable light, whom no one has ever seen or can see; to him be honor and eternal dominion.   1 TIMOTHY 6:15–16 NRSV

But He said, "You cannot see My face; for no man shall see Me, and live."   EXODUS 33:20 NKJV

God is physically unapproachable; our physical nature is too fragile to bear the tremendous glory and brilliance of His presence.

And the Lord continued, "See, there is a place by me where you shall stand on the rock; and while my glory passes by I will put you in a cleft of the rock, and I will cover you with my hand until I have passed by; then I will take away my hand, and you shall see my back; but my face shall not be seen."   EXODUS 33:21–23 NRSV

However, for those who are in Christ Jesus, God is spiritually approachable:

Let us then approach the throne of grace with confidence, so that we may receive mercy and find grace to help us in our time of need.   HEBREWS 4:16 NIV

In him *(Christ Jesus)* and through faith in him we may approach God with freedom and confidence.

EPHESIANS 3:12 NIV

Unchanging
See "Immutable."

"For I am the Lord, I do not change."

MALACHI 3:6 NKJV

"You, Lord, in the beginning laid the foundation of the earth, And the heavens are the work of Your hands; They will perish, but You remain; And they will all grow old like a garment; Like a cloak You will fold them up, And they will be changed. But You are the same, And Your years will not fail."

HEBREWS 1:10–12, NKJV

Every generous act of giving, with every perfect gift, is from above, coming down from the Father of lights, with whom there is no variation or shadow due to change.   JAMES 1:17 NRSV

Unfailing

Your love, O LORD, reaches to the heavens, your faithfulness to the skies. Your righteousness is like the mighty mountains, your justice like the great deep. . . . How priceless is your unfailing love!   PSALM 36:5–7 NIV

"Blessed be the Lord, who has given rest to His people Israel, according to all that He promised. There has not failed one word of all His good promise."

1 KINGS 8:56 NKJV

The LORD's delight is in those who honor him, those who put their hope in his unfailing love.

PSALM 147:11 NLT

Many sorrows come to the wicked, but unfailing love surrounds those who trust the LORD. So rejoice in the LORD and be glad, all you who obey him! Shout for joy, all you whose hearts are pure!   PSALM 32:10–11 NLT

Unfathomable

Oh, the depth of the riches both of the wisdom and knowledge of God! How unsearchable are His judgments and His ways past finding out!

ROMANS 11:33 NKJV

Great is the LORD and most worthy of praise; his greatness no one can fathom.   PSALM 145:3 NIV

He has made everything beautiful in its time. He has also set eternity in the hearts of men; yet they cannot fathom what God has done from beginning to end.

ECCLESIASTES 3:11 NIV

Unforgetting

For God is true, and will not put away from him the memory of your work and of your love for his name, in the help which you gave and still give to the saints.

HEBREWS 6:10 BBE

"I *(the Lord)* will never forget anything they have done."
AMOS 8:7 NIV

The Lord, however, deliberately chooses to remove from His memory the sins of those who have received Jesus as their Savior and Lord.

"I, even I, am He who blots out your transgressions for My own sake; And I will not remember your sins."
ISAIAH 43:25 NKJV

"For I will be merciful to their unrighteousness, and their sins and their lawless deeds I will remember no more."
HEBREWS 8:12 NKJV

"Can a mother forget the baby at her breast and have no compassion on the child she has borne? Though she may forget, I will not forget you!"
ISAIAH 49:15 NIV

Unimaginable

And I pray that. . .you be able to feel and understand, as all God's children should, how long, how wide, how deep, and how high his love really is; and to experience this love for yourselves, though it is so great that you will never see the end of it or fully know or understand it. . . . God who by his mighty power at work within us is able to do far more than we would ever dare to ask or

203

even dream of—infinitely beyond our highest prayers, desires, thoughts, or hopes.   EPHESIANS 3:17–20 TLB

"No eye has seen, no ear has heard, and no mind has imagined what God has prepared for those who love him."   1 CORINTHIANS 2:9 NLT

Unique

"Before Me there was no God formed, Nor shall there be after Me. I, even I, am the Lord, And besides Me there is no savior."   ISAIAH 43:10–11 NKJV

No one has ever seen God. It is God the only Son *(Jesus)*, who is close to the Father's heart, who has made him known.   JOHN 1:18 NRSV

God, the blessed and only Ruler, the King of kings and Lord of lords, who alone is immortal and who lives in unapproachable light, whom no one has seen or can see. To Him be honor and might forever.

1 TIMOTHY 6:15–16 NIV

" 'For this time I will send all my plagues upon you yourself, and upon your officials, and upon your people, so that you may know that there is no one like me in all the earth.' "   EXODUS 9:14 NRSV

"Who is like you, O Lord, among the gods? Who is like you, majestic in holiness, awesome in splendor, doing wonders?"   EXODUS 15:11 NRSV

There is none like God, O Jeshurun, who rides through the heavens to your help, majestic through the skies.

DEUTERONOMY 33:26 NRSV

"Therefore You are great, O Lord God. For there is none like You, nor is there any God besides You, according to all that we have heard with our ears."

2 SAMUEL 7:22 NKJV

To whom will ye liken me, and make me equal, and compare me, that we may be like? I am God, and there is none else; I am God, and there is none like me. Declaring the end from the beginning, and from ancient times the things that are not yet done, saying, My counsel shall stand, and I will do all my pleasure.

ISAIAH 46:5, 9–10 KJV

Unity
See "Trinity."

"The Lord our God, the Lord is one!"

DEUTERONOMY 6:4 NKJV

Unsearchable

"Can you fathom the mysteries of God? Can you probe the limits of the Almighty? They are higher than the heavens—what can you do? They are deeper than the depths of the grave—what can you know? Their measure is longer than the earth and wider than the sea."

JOB 11:7–9 NIV

Upright
See "Just" and "Righteous."

The LORD is good and does what is right; he shows the proper path to those who go astray. He leads the humble in what is right, teaching them his way. The LORD leads with unfailing love and faithfulness all those who keep his covenant and obey his decrees.

PSALM 25:8–10 NLT

For the LORD is righteous, he loves righteous deeds; the upright shall behold his face.   PSALM 11:7 RSV

Showing that the Lord is upright; he is my rock, and there is no unrighteousness in him.

PSALM 92:15 NRSV

These six things doth the LORD hate: yea, seven are an abomination unto him: A proud look, a lying tongue, and hands that shed innocent blood, An heart that deviseth wicked imaginations, feet that be swift in running to mischief, A false witness that speaketh lies, and he that soweth discord among brethren.

PROVERBS 6:16–19 KJV

"The fear of the LORD is hatred of evil. Pride and arrogance and the way of evil and perverted speech I hate."

PROVERBS 8:13 RSV

Victorious

He *(God)* holds victory in store for the upright, he is a shield to those whose walk is blameless.

PROVERBS 2:7 NIV

"It is the Lord your God who goes with you, to fight for you against your enemies, to give you victory."

DEUTERONOMY 20:4 NRSV

The horse is made ready for the day of battle, but victory rests with the LORD.

PROVERBS 21:31 NIV

You have also given me the shield of Your salvation; Your right hand has held me up, Your gentleness has made me great.

PSALM 18:35 NKJV

"With God are wisdom and strength; he has counsel and understanding. If he tears down, no one can rebuild; if he shuts someone in, no one can open up. If he withholds the waters, they dry up; if he sends them out, they overwhelm the land. With him are strength and wisdom; the deceived and the deceiver are his."

JOB 12:13–16 NRSV

For not by their own sword did they win the land, nor did their own arm give them victory; but your right hand, and your arm, and the light of your countenance, for you delighted in them.   PSALM 44:3 NRSV

"The LORD, your God, is in your midst, a warrior who gives victory; he will rejoice over you with gladness, he will renew you in his love; he will exult over you with loud singing."   ZEPHANIAH 3:17 RSV

I do not trust in my bow, my sword does not bring me victory; but you give us victory over our enemies, you put our adversaries to shame.   PSALM 44:6–7 NIV

Through God we will do valiantly, For it is He who shall tread down our enemies.   PSALM 60:12 NKJV

Shouts of joy and victory resound in the tents of the righteous: "The LORD's right hand has done mighty things!"   PSALM 118:15 NIV

Thanks be to God, who gives us the victory through our Lord Jesus Christ.   1 CORINTHIANS 15:57 RSV

This is love for God: to obey his commands. And his commands are not burdensome, for everyone born of God overcomes the world. This is the victory that has overcome the world, even our faith. Who is it that overcomes the world? Only he who believes that Jesus is the Son of God.   1 JOHN 5:3–5 NIV

Virtuous
See "Good," "True," "Worthy of Praise."

The fruit of the Spirit is love, joy, peace, patience, kindness, generosity, faithfulness, gentleness, and self-control.   GALATIANS 5:22–23 NRSV

For God did not give us a spirit of fear, but of power and of love and of self-control.   2 TIMOTHY 1:7 BBE

Wise

For God's foolishness is wiser than human wisdom, and God's weakness is stronger than human strength.
    1 CORINTHIANS 1:25 NRSV

Daniel answered and said, Blessed be the name of God for ever and ever: for wisdom and might are his: And he changeth the times and the seasons: he removeth kings, and setteth up kings: he giveth wisdom unto the wise, and knowledge to them that know understanding: He revealeth the deep and secret things: he knoweth what is in the darkness, and the light dwelleth with him.

DANIEL 2:20–22 KJV

It is he who made the earth by his power, who established the world by his wisdom, and by his understanding stretched out the heavens.   JEREMIAH 10:12 RSV

"Truly, your God is God of gods and Lord of kings, and a revealer of mysteries."   DANIEL 2:47 RSV

My son, if you receive my words and treasure up my commandments with you, making your ear attentive to wisdom and inclining your heart to understanding; yes, if you cry out for insight and raise your voice for understanding, if you seek it like silver and search for it as for hidden treasures; then you will understand the fear of the LORD and find the knowledge of God. For the LORD gives wisdom; from his mouth come knowledge and understanding.   PROVERBS 2:1–6 RSV

To the only wise God, through Jesus Christ, be the glory for ever.   ROMANS 16:27 BBE

Let no man deceive himself. If any man among you seemeth to be wise in this world, let him become a fool, that he may be wise. For the wisdom of this world is foolishness with God. For it is written, He taketh the wise in their own craftiness. And again, The Lord knoweth the thoughts of the wise, that they are vain. Therefore let no man glory in men.

1 CORINTHIANS 3:18–21 KJV

Reverence for the LORD is the foundation of true wisdom. The rewards of wisdom come to all who obey him. PSALM 111:10 NLT

Wonderful

His name will be called Wonderful, Counselor, Mighty God, Everlasting Father, Prince of Peace.

ISAIAH 9:6 NKJV

This also comes from the Lord of hosts, Who is wonderful in counsel and excellent in guidance.

ISAIAH 28:29 NKJV

Blessed be the Lord, for he has wondrously shown his steadfast love to me when I was beset as a city under siege. PSALM 31:21 NRSV

Your laws are wonderful; no wonder I obey them.

PSALM 119:129 TLB

Oh, that men would give thanks to the Lord for His goodness, And for His wonderful works to the children of men! PSALM 107:15 NKJV

On the glorious splendor of your majesty, and on your wondrous works, I will meditate. The might of your awesome deeds shall be proclaimed, and I will declare your greatness. They shall celebrate the fame of your abundant goodness, and shall sing aloud of your righteousness. PSALM 145:5–7 NRSV

. . .that you *(the followers of Jesus)* may show to others how God called you out of the darkness into his wonderful light. 1 PETER 2:9 TLB

Word

In the beginning the Word already existed. He was with God, and he was God. JOHN 1:1 NLT

For the word of God is living and powerful, and sharper than any two-edged sword, piercing even to the division of soul and spirit, and of joints and marrow, and is a discerner of the thoughts and intents of the heart. HEBREWS 4:12 NKJV

By the word of the LORD were the heavens made; and all the host of them by the breath of his mouth. He gathereth the waters of the sea together as an heap: he layeth up the depth in storehouses. Let all the earth fear the LORD: let all the inhabitants of the world stand in awe of him. For he spake, and it was done; he commanded, and it stood fast.   PSALM 33:6–9 KJV

"Is not My word like a fire?" says the Lord, "And like a hammer that breaks the rock in pieces?"

JEREMIAH 23:29 NKJV

For you have been born again. Your new life did not come from your earthly parents because the life they gave you will end in death. But this new life will last forever because it comes from the eternal, living word of God.   1 PETER 1:23 NLT

"All men are like grass, and all their glory is like the flowers of the field; the grass withers and the flowers fall, but the word of the Lord stands forever."

1 PETER 1:24–25 NIV

By God's Word, He has done or will do each of the following:

Create: Let all the earth fear the Lord; let all the inhabitants of the world stand in awe of him. For he spoke, and it came to be; he commanded, and it stood firm.

PSALM 33:8–9 NRSV

Hold together: The Son is the radiance of God's glory and the exact representation of his being, sustaining all things by his powerful Word.   HEBREWS 1:3 NIV

Destroy: But by the same word the present heavens and earth have been reserved for fire, being kept until the day of judgment and destruction of the godless.

2 PETER 3:7 NRSV

Re-create: But having faith in his word, we are looking for a new heaven and a new earth, which will be the resting-place of righteousness.   2 PETER 3:13 BBE

Worthy of Praise

Finally, beloved, whatever is true, whatever is honorable, whatever is just, whatever is pure, whatever is pleasing, whatever is commendable, if there is any excellence and if there is anything worthy of praise, think about these things.   PHILIPPIANS 4:8 NRSV

Philippians 4:8 is an instruction to us, but it describes God!

But the wisdom that is from above is first pure, then peaceable, gentle, willing to yield, full of mercy and good fruits, without partiality and without hypocrisy.

JAMES 3:17 NKJV

Give unto the Lord the glory due to His name; Worship the Lord in the beauty of holiness.

PSALM 29:2 NKJV

Great is the LORD and most worthy of praise; his greatness no one can fathom.   PSALM 145:3 NIV

In a great chorus they sang, "Holy, holy, holy is the LORD Almighty! The whole earth is filled with his glory!"   ISAIAH 6:3 NLT

"You are worthy, O Lord, To receive glory and honor and power; For You created all things, And by Your will they exist and were created."   REVELATION 4:11 NKJV

"I call upon the LORD, who is worthy to be praised, and I am saved from my enemies."   2 SAMUEL 22:4 RSV

Give thanks unto the LORD, call upon his name, make known his deeds among the people. Sing unto him, sing psalms unto him, talk ye of all his wondrous works. Glory ye in his holy name: let the heart of them rejoice that seek the LORD. Seek the LORD and his strength, seek his face continually. Remember his marvellous works that he hath done, his wonders, and the judgments of his mouth.   1 CHRONICLES 16:8–12 KJV

This is the word of the Lord: Let not the wise man take pride in his wisdom, or the strong man in his strength, or the man of wealth in his wealth: But if any man has pride, let it be in this, that he has the wisdom to have knowledge of me, that I am the Lord, working mercy, giving true decisions, and doing righteousness in the earth: for in these things I have delight, says the Lord.

JEREMIAH 9:23–24 BBE

Thy kingdom is an everlasting kingdom, and thy dominion endureth throughout all generations. The LORD upholdeth all that fall, and raiseth up all those that be bowed down. The eyes of all wait upon thee; and thou givest them their meat in due season. Thou openest thine hand, and satisfiest the desire of every living thing. The LORD is righteous in all his ways, and holy in all his works. The LORD is nigh unto all them that call upon him, to all that call upon him in truth. He will fulfil the desire of them that fear him: he also will hear their cry, and will save them. The LORD preserveth all them that love him: but all the wicked will he destroy. My mouth shall speak the praise of the LORD: and let all flesh bless his holy name for ever and ever.   PSALM 145:13–21 KJV

For great is the LORD and most worthy of praise; he is to be feared above all gods. For all the gods of the nations are idols, but the LORD made the heavens. Splendor and majesty are before him; strength and joy in his dwelling place.   1 CHRONICLES 16:25–27 NIV

O worship the LORD in the beauty of holiness: fear before him, all the earth. Say among the heathen that the Lord reigneth: the world also shall be established that it shall not be moved: he shall judge the people righteously. Let the heavens rejoice, and let the earth be glad; let the sea roar, and the fulness thereof. Let the field be joyful, and all that is therein: then shall all the trees of the wood rejoice Before the LORD: for he cometh, for he cometh to judge the earth: he shall judge the world with righteousness, and the people with his truth.   PSALM 96:9–13 KJV

Praise ye the LORD. Praise God in his sanctuary: praise him in the firmament of his power. Praise him for his mighty acts: praise him according to his excellent greatness. Praise him with the sound of the trumpet: praise him with the psaltery and harp. Praise him with the timbrel and dance: praise him with stringed instruments and organs. Praise him upon the loud cymbals: praise him upon the high sounding cymbals. Let every thing that hath breath praise the LORD. Praise ye the LORD.   PSALM 150:1–6 KJV

Xristos
See "Christ."

Xristos is Greek for Christ.

"We have found the Messiah" (which is translated, the Christ).   JOHN 1:41 NKJV

Messiah means Ruler.

"He is the Christ, the chosen of God." LUKE 23:35 NKJV

Now may our Lord Jesus Christ himself and God our Father, who loved us and through grace gave us eternal comfort and good hope, comfort your hearts and strengthen them in every good work and word.
2 THESSALONIANS 2:16–17 NRSV

Yearning (for us)

The Lord is not slow in keeping his promise, as some understand slowness. He is patient with you, not wanting anyone to perish, but everyone to come to repentance.   2 PETER 3:9 NIV

O Ephraim *(put your name in place of Ephraim)*, what have I to do with idols? It is I who answer and look after you. I am like an evergreen cypress; your faithfulness comes from me.   HOSEA 14:8 NRSV

The LORD longs to be gracious to you.

ISAIAH 30:18 NIV

"Is not Ephraim my dear son, the child in whom I delight? Though I often speak against him *(because he repeatedly sins and commits adultery against the Lord),* I still remember him. Therefore my heart yearns for him; I have great compassion for him," declares the LORD.

JEREMIAH 31:20 NIV

" 'How gladly would I treat you like sons and give you a desirable land, the most beautiful inheritance of any nation.' I thought you would call me 'Father' and not turn away from following me."

JEREMIAH 3:19 NIV

"If you had responded to my rebuke, I would have poured out my heart to you and made my thoughts known to you."

PROVERBS 1:23 NIV

"And when I passed by you, and saw you weltering in your blood, I said to you. . .'Live.' "

EZEKIEL 16:6 RSV

"Listen! I am standing at the door, knocking; if you hear my voice and open the door, I will come in to you and eat with you, and you with me."

REVELATION 3:20 NRSV

Zealous

"I *(the Lord)* will. . .punish those who are complacent, . . .who think, 'The LORD will do nothing, either good or bad.' Their blood will be poured out like dust and their entrails like filth. Neither their silver nor their gold will be able to save them on the day of the LORD's wrath."   ZEPHANIAH 1:12, 17–18 NIV

Yea, truth faileth; and he that departeth from evil maketh himself a prey: and the LORD saw it, and it displeased him that there was no judgment. And he saw that there was no man, and wondered that there was no intercessor: therefore his arm brought salvation unto him; and his righteousness, it sustained him. For he put on righteousness as a breastplate, and an helmet of salvation upon his head; and he put on the garments of vengeance for clothing, and was clad with zeal as a cloak. According to their deeds, accordingly he will repay, fury to his adversaries, recompence to his enemies; to the islands he will repay recompence.

ISAIAH 59:15–18 KJV

"Phinehas. . .has turned my anger away from the Israelites; for he was as zealous as I *(the Lord)* am for my honor among them, so that in my zeal I did not put an end to them."   NUMBERS 25:11 NIV

"This is what the Sovereign LORD says: . . .I will be zealous for my holy name."   EZEKIEL 39:25 NIV

His authority shall grow continually, and there shall be endless peace. . . He will establish and uphold it with justice and with righteousness from this time onward and forevermore. The zeal of the Lord of hosts will do this.   ISAIAH 9:7 NRSV

And I am convinced that nothing can ever separate us from his *(God's)* love. Death can't, and life can't. The angels can't, and the demons can't. Our fears for today, our worries about tomorrow, and even the powers of hell can't keep God's love away. Whether we are high above the sky or in the deepest ocean, nothing in all creation will ever be able to separate us from the love of God that is revealed in Christ Jesus our Lord.

ROMANS 8:38–39 NLT

Author's Note

This list of God's attributes and this list of references can never be complete—God is infinite and there is infinitely more about which to praise the holy, one and only, Lord our God.

Love the LORD your God
with all your heart
and with all your soul
and with all your strength.
DEUTERONOMY 6:5 NIV

Who among the gods is like you, O LORD?
Who is like you—majestic in holiness,
awesome in glory, working wonders?
EXODUS 15:11 NIV

Inspirational Library

Beautiful purse/pocket-size editions of Christian classics bound in flexible leatherette. These books make thoughtful gifts for everyone on your list, including yourself!

When I'm on My Knees　　The highly popular collection of devotional thoughts on prayer, especially for women.
　　Flexible Leatherette. $4.97

The Bible Promise Book　　Over 1,000 promises from God's Word arranged by topic. What does God promise about matters like: Anger, Illness, Jealousy, Love, Money, Old Age, and Mercy? Find out in this book!
　　Flexible Leatherette. $3.97

Daily Wisdom for Women　　A daily devotional for women seeking biblical wisdom to apply to their lives. Scripture taken from the New American Standard Version of the Bible.
　　Flexible Leatherette. $4.97

My Daily Prayer Journal　　Each page is dated and features a Scripture verse and ample room for you to record your thoughts, prayers, and praises. One page for each day of the year.
　　Flexible Leatherette. $4.97

Available wherever books are sold.
Or order from:

Barbour Publishing, Inc.
P.O. Box 719
Uhrichsville, OH 44683
http://www.barbourbooks.com

If you order by mail, add $2.00 to your order for shipping.
Prices are subject to change without notice.